Applying
Kingdom
Education™

Following God's Instructions for Educating Future Generations

Glen Schultz

Applying Kingdom Education™
Following God's Instructions for Educating Future Generations

© 2021 by Glen Schultz

Published by Wheaton Press
Wheaton, Illinois
www.WheatonPress.com

ISBN-10: 1-950258-42-4
ISBN-13: 978-1-950258-42-0 (WheatonPress.com)

Scripture taken from the New King James Version®. Copyright © 1982 by Thomas Nelson. Used by permission. All rights reserved.

Go to www.WheatonPress.com to learn about additional resources.

Contents

In memory of Dr. Roy Lowrie, Jr.

Dr. Lowrie was one of the first persons to challenge me to think about all of life from a biblical perspective. His application of Scripture marked his ministry and left an indelible mark on my life. Once, when I shared an object lesson with him to get his approval, he replied, "Remember, only God's Word is inspired." Those words have guided me throughout my ministry and as I wrote this book.

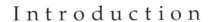

Introduction

Behold, children are a heritage from the
Lord: the fruit of the womb is a reward.
PSALM 127:3

*If I profess with the loudest voice and clearest exposition
every portion of the Word of God except precisely that little
point which the world and the devil are at that moment
attacking, I am not confessing Christ, however boldly I
may be professing Him. Where the battle rages, the loyalty
of the solider is proved; and to be steady on all the battle
front besides, is mere flight and disgrace if he flinches at
that point.*[1]

Martin Luther

IT'S NOT A SECRET that there is a cultural battle for hearts
and minds of future generations happening across our educational
systems. The invitation and temptation to conform to a cultural mold
that is contrary to the reflection of Christ is a battle that our students
are confronted with from their earliest days of child development to
the highest echelons of our educational institutions. The question

---

1   Martin Luther, "Quotes," https://www.goodreads.com/
quotes/657155-if-i-profess-with-the-loudest-voice-and-clearest-exposition.

that we are faced with answering is not whether or not "if" the battle exists, but whether or not the Body of Christ is willing to step into the battle without flinching and address the issue of education biblically.

If we are not willing to address the issue of education biblically, then it doesn't matter how we fight on other issues. We will be left to flee in disgrace, and generations will pay the price for our failure. In the companion book to this resource, *Understanding Kingdom Education: A Challenge to the Home, Church and School*, I lay out the case for Kingdom Education™.

Scripture makes it clear that embracing a Christ-centered, Bible-based philosophy of education is the responsibility of every Christian. Individuals, families, churches, and schools must each commit and own their responsibility to educate each generation from a Christ-centered, Bible-based philosophy of education.

Deuteronomy 6 and Psalms 78 and 127 are just a few passages of Scripture where God instructs parents that they have the primary responsibility to educate children and youth according to God's instructions. Psalm 127:3 tells parents that their children are a *heritage of the Lord*. This phrase can be paraphrased, *behold, children are God's homework assignment to parents*. (This concept is fully described in my first book *Kingdom Education™*.)

Since children are God's homework assignment to parents, it is vital that parents understand how God expects us to complete His assignment. Thankfully, we are not left to our own ideas, concepts, or creations to meet the expectation. God's Word provides us with specific principles that when applied equip parents to successfully make disciples of Jesus Christ of each new generation.

The church and the school must partner with the home to assist parents in accomplishing the task of educating future generations according to God's plan. God's plan is that parents, pastors, and teachers must each know, understand, and commit to the biblical principles of Kingdom Education™.

It is one thing to know these principles. But it is another thing to understand them to the point of being able to put them into practice throughout the entire educational process. If parents, church leaders, and educators do not partner together and embody these principles with intentionality and integrity, then Kingdom Education™ loses credibility.

In the classic book by Kouzes and Posner, *Credibility*, they reported that three practices had to be taking place on a continual basis if an individual or organization is going to maintain credibility.

The first practice Kouzes and Posner identified was to clarify our beliefs.

Twenty years ago when *Kingdom Education™: God's Plan for Educating Future Generations* was released, it laid the foundation for a clear biblical philosophy of education by outlining the roles of the home, church, and school regarding God's design for educating a child.

The second required practice identified by Kouzes and Posner to maintain and build credibility is the need to unify everyone involved. Credible organizations and people know where they are going, how they are going to get there, and what principles are going to guide them.

In book two of this series, *Understanding Kingdom Education™: A Challenge to the Home, Church and School*, I took the foundational beliefs outlined in the first book and presented our need as Christians to unify around the biblical principles of Kingdom Education™.

In the foreword to my original book, Josh McDowell wrote,

> *The ideal way to help our kids not only to reject the postmodern worldview but also embrace deepened Christian convictions is to align church, home and school into a unified whole that arms our children with the truth and protects them from distortions.*

Individual Christians, parents, church leaders, and educators must each "align ourselves into a unified whole" when it comes to how children are educated. Regardless of our role in the process, each of us as believers must understand the principles of Kingdom Education™ to guide us as we carry out the divine mandate to educate future generations biblically.

The third principle from Kouzes and Posner that must be present for credibility to reach full capacity is intensifying all of our actions. According to their research, this particular aspect of credibility is of utmost importance. For us to operate at full strength, Christians must be committed to the principles of Kingdom Education™ to the point that there is consistency between our words and our actions. Achieving this level of credibility and authenticity is the goal of this third resource in the Kingdom Education™ series.

While it is important to clarify the foundational beliefs of Kingdom Education™, it is equally important to know God's instructions regarding how to educate our children and to understand the educational principles that are set forth in Scripture. However, we must also take the final step if we are going to be successful in raising future generations to know God and are equipped to think and act from a biblical worldview. There must be consistency between knowing the biblical principles of Kingdom Education™ in our minds and practicing them in our home, our church, and our school through the entire educational process.

This third resource presents each of the 14 biblical principles of Kingdom Education™ in detail for this purpose of challenging us to move beyond beliefs and values and into the authentic application and implementation of each principle so that we can live and reflect lives of credibility.

At the end of each chapter are questions and exercises that invite you to reflect and respond to what you have read as you apply the principles to your own life and circles of influence. Whether you are reading this as a single parent or a solo educator, I invite and encourage you to find a group where you can encourage each other as you contemplate the implications and consider the application to your circles of influence.

Our goal is that what we post on our walls regarding our beliefs and philosophy of Christ-centered, Bible-based education can be observed by our students as we live our lives in front of them daily at home, church, and school.

Chapter 1

Who Owns the Children?

The most important Christian Education
institution is not the pulpit or the school,
important as those institutions are; but it is the
Christian family. And that institution has to a
very large extent ceased to do its work.[2]
J. GRESHAM MACHEN

A QUESTION THAT EVERY PARENT is eventually confronted with is who owns our children. To most parents, the seemingly obvious answer is that parents own their children. However, this belief is not the consensus perspective in our current culture.

---

2   John Gresham Machen. *AZQuotes.com* (Wind and Fly LTD, 2021). https://www.azquotes.com/quote/1430333, accessed 2021.

Author, professor, and political commentator Dr. Melissa Harris-Perry shared her perspective during an interview on MSNBC:

> *We have never invested as much in public education as we should have because we've always had kind of a private notion of children. Your kid is yours and totally your responsibility. We haven't had a very collective notion of these are our children. So part of it is we have to **break through our kind of private idea that kids belong to their parents** or kids belong to their families and **recognize that kids belong to whole communities**. Once it's everyone's responsibility and not just the household's, then we start making better investments.*[3]

Harris-Perry's statement that children belong to the "community" is not new. The African proverb that states, *it takes a village to raise a child* was paraphrased to become the title of book written by former US Senator and First Lady of the United States, Hillary Clinton.

At first glance, the concept of children belonging to the "village" or "whole communities" seems innocuous but history reveals a series of natural consequences that begin to emerge from this philosophy of education. Whenever a society believes that it owns the children, it then declares and demands that it has the right and the responsibility to educate children in whatever way that society deems best.

This is not something new. One can go back to the time when the nation of Israel was taken into Babylonian captivity. Nebuchadnezzar, king of Babylon, wanted to make sure that the young Israelites were

---

3   Melissa Harris-Perry, InspiringQuotes.us, https://www.inspiringquotes.us/quotes/ZU3h_xOJPWgoz.

educated in a way that would cause them to forget God and His Word and be fit to serve the king. In Daniel 1:3-5, we find these words:

> *Then the king instructed Ashpenaz, the master of his eunuchs, to bring some of the children of Israel and some of the king's descendants and some of the nobles, young men in whom there was no blemish, but good-looking, gifted in wisdom, possessing knowledge and quick to understand, who had ability to serve in the king's palace, and whom they might teach the language and literature of the Chaldeans. And the king appointed for them a daily provision of the king's delicacies and of the wine which he drank, and **three years of training for them**, so that at the end of that time they might **serve before the king**.*

Throughout the annals of history, one can find various individuals and governments who claimed the right to educate the children according to their beliefs and values. Some examples include the following quotes:

> *The education of all children, from the moment that they can get along without a mother's care, shall be in state institutions.*[4]
>
> *Karl Marx*

> *Give me four years to teach the children and the seed that I have sown will never be uprooted.*[5]
>
> *Vladimir Lenin*

---

4   Karl Marx, https://www.inspiringquotes.us/author/6212-karl-marx/about-children.

5   Vladimir Lenin, https://www.brainyquote.com/quotes/vladimir_lenin_153238.

We who are engaged in the sacred cause of education are entitled to look upon all parents as having given hostages (their children) to our cause.[6]

Horace Mann

The youth of today is ever the people of tomorrow. For this reason, we have set before ourselves the task of inoculating our youth with the spirit of this community of the people at a very early age, at an age when human beings are still unperverted and therefore unspoiled. This Reich stands, and it is building itself up for the future, upon its youth. And this new Reich will give its youth to no one, but will itself take youth and give to youth its own education and its own up bringing.[7]

Adolf Hitler

In Irwin Lutzer's book *When a Nation Forgets God*, he describes how Hitler seized ownership of all the youth of Germany. Lutzer explained how Hitler used his authority to educate the children and youth in line with the principles of the new Reich.

Parents had the responsibility of raising the child's body meaning what the child ate was decided by the parents. The Reich would educate the child's soul, meaning what the child believed and felt was the responsibility of the Reich.[8]

---

6   Horace Mann, https://quotefancy.com/quote/1004900/Horace-Mann-We-who-are-engaged-in-the-sacred-cause-of-education-are-entitled-to-look-upon.

7   Erwin W. Lutzer, *When a Nation Forgets God* (Chicago: Moody Publishers, 2010), 99.

8   Ibid. 103.

This belief of ownership of children and youth by the government stands in stark opposition to the teaching of the Scriptures, and leads us to our first biblical principle of Kingdom Education™.

Biblical Principle of Kingdom Education™ #1
The education of children and youth is the primary responsibility of parents.

> *Behold, children are a heritage from the Lord.*
>
> *Psalm 127:3*

> *You shall teach them diligently to your children, and shall talk of them when you sit in your house, when you walk by the way, when you lie down, and when you rise up. You shall bind them as a sign on your hand, and they shall be as frontlets between your eyes. You shall write them on the doorposts of your house and on your gates.*
>
> *Deuteronomy 6:7-9*

> *You shall teach them to your children, speaking of them when you sit in your house, when you walk by the way, when you lie down, and when you rise up.*
>
> *Deuteronomy 11:19*

> *We will not hide them from their children, telling to the generation to come the praises of the Lord, and His strength and His wonderful works that He has done. For He established a testimony in Jacob, and appointed a law in Israel, which He commanded our fathers, that they should make them known to their children;*
>
> *Psalm 78:4-5*

Train up a child in the way he should go: and when he is old, he will not depart from it.

Proverbs 22:6

But did He not make them one, having a remnant of the Spirit? And why one? He seeks godly offspring.

Malachi 2:15

And you, fathers, do not provoke your children to wrath, but bring them up in the training and admonition of the Lord.

Ephesians 6:4

These passages represent just a few of the ones found in the Bible that make it clear that children belong to the parents. When I say that children belong to their parents, I mean that God gives children to parents, and the parents are responsible to raise them in line with God's Word and educate their children biblically. While most of the instruction to parents about this responsibility is specifically given to fathers, both parents are to play a significant role in educating their children. Solomon admonished his sons to listen to the instruction of their mother.

My son, hear the instruction of thy father, and forsake not the law of thy mother

Proverbs 1:8

Two questions we must ask are the following:

1. *Do we as parents understand our responsibility for educating our children biblically?*
2. *Are parents accepting this responsibility?*

Several years ago, the Barna Group conducted a research project to determine if and how parents understood their God-given responsibilities of raising their children. The results were alarming.

- *87%* of Christian parents believed that they were responsible for the *spiritual and moral development* of their children.
- Only 33% of born-again parents claimed the church and faith were important influences on their parenting ideas and actions.
- *Less than half* of Christian parents mentioned anything related to their faith (including the Bible, church, or religion) as significant influences on how they raise their children.

At first glance, 87% seems rather encouraging. However, it must be noted that the 87% of parents mentioned believed that they were ***only*** responsible for the ***spiritual and moral development*** of their children. This does not indicate that they believed they are responsible for the entire education of their children. But that isn't the divine assignment entrusted by God to parents. We are responsible for the head, heart, and hands of our children, not just portions of each.

Parents who desire to raise Christ-centered children must first understand and follow the principle that tells them they are responsible for the education their children receive—be it at home, church, or school.

Psalm 127:3 states that children are a *heritage of the Lord*. However, most fail to understand what the phrase *a heritage of the Lord* really means. I believe that it can be paraphrased this way.

Children: God's Homework Assignment to Parents!

We all understand homework assignments. When we were given homework assignments from our teachers, we knew that it was our responsibility to complete them thoroughly. Every assignment was eventually graded by the teacher, and whatever grade we received was based on how well we completed the assignment.

It is not enough to merely know that we, as parents, are responsible for the education our children receive. We must also understand how God views this responsibility. In the second chapter of Malachi, God was not paying attention to the sacrifices of His people. The people were actually weeping over the altar and asking God why He was not regarding their religious sacrifices.

The reason that God was not regarding His people's "religious activity" was because their homes were a mess and divorce was rampant. God explained how He had ordained husband and wife to become one flesh for one ultimate purpose. God wanted to get "godly seed" from the marriage relationship. This is the same thing He wants from parents today. God wants and expects Christian parents to produce godly offspring.

The problem facing today's parents is that many of us have unintentionally or unknowingly abdicated something that is our God-given responsibility. Statistics don't lie. Too many of us have given the primary responsibility of educating their children over to others—mainly the government or the state. This was not always the case here in the United States. Historian, Francis Curran, found that what had taken place is

> …a revolutionary development in the history of education and in the history of Christianity: The surrender by American Protestantism during the past century of the control of popular elementary education to the state… Only in the United States has Protestantism relinquished the traditional claim of the Christian church [parents] to

exercise control over the formal education of its children in the elementary school…The Christian churches eventually agreed that the state must have an important place in the direction of popular elementary education.[9]

Curran understood that when Christians gave the responsibility of educating children in the elementary grades to the state, it would have far reaching implications to all levels of education.

…if a church withdraws from one division of education, the logical consequence of that withdrawal will be the ultimate abandonment of all formal education by that church.[10]

Of course, this is exactly where we are in today's culture. The vast majority of parents believe that the public "school," which is the state, should be responsible for what children are taught. The home and church need to focus on teaching children faith and values and the school must teach the facts or the "academics."

Psalm 78:1-7 is a very important passage for all parents to read and study. The Psalmist explained how parents in general and fathers specifically must diligently teach their children the things of God. The passage indicates that parents must have a long-range vision when it comes to educating their children. In fact, four generations of people are referenced in these few verses.

I compare this passage and its meaning to running a relay race. Of all the events in track and field, the 4 by 100-meter relay race is one of the

---

9   Francis Curran, *The Churches and Schools: American Protestantism and Popular Elementary Education* (Chicago: Loyola University Press, 1954), Preface.

10   Curran, *The Churches and Schools*, 5.

most exciting to watch. Here, four men or women take their places 100 meters apart around the track. At the sound of the gun, the first runner explodes out of the blocks expending all his/her energy in an effort to get to the next runner.

As the first runner, with baton in hand, approaches the second runner, the second person begins running away. Tension builds as the first runner must not only catch the next runner but must also successfully pass the baton to this teammate. The baton must be passed within a set length of the track or the team is disqualified. The same is true if the baton is dropped—the race is over.

As the second runner attempts to pass the baton to the third runner and the same thing takes place with the fourth runner, the first runner doesn't simply relax. He/she continues to be engaged in the race. But now, the first runner can only pray that each runner is successful in passing the baton. The same involvement holds true for each runner until the race is over.

Once the baton has been successfully passed to all four runners and the last runner crosses the finish line, the entire team can rejoice for completing the race. This analogy can easily be applied to what we find in the first seven verses of Psalm 78.

Every Christian parent is involved in a similar race, but the stakes in this race are far greater than any other relay ever run. This race determines whether or not our children attain a prize that will last for all eternity. As each successive generation enters the race, the effort of the first parents becomes increasingly more important.

The baton in this race is our faith in Christ—not carried in the hand but in the heart. The goal is to pass the baton of faith from the parents' heart to the child's heart. It is critical that every Christian trains and prepares before entering the parenting race, toning spiritual muscles into peak condition.

As the birth of the first child draws closer, parents are set in the starting blocks, readying themselves for the starter's pistol. With their spiritual lives coiled for action, they must explode out of the blocks the moment birth take place. This is so critical because as soon as a child is delivered, he starts running away from his parents—it's called growing up. Every parent eventually says that the child grew up too fast. You have heard them say, "It seems like only yesterday that we were bringing him home from the hospital, and now he is going out into life on his own."

From birth on, the parents must expend all of their energy to accomplish one goal—passing on their faith to their child's heart. They must stretch and strain to get the baton firmly in the grasp of their child's heart before the child gets too far down the racetrack of life. Statistics show that the odds of an individual placing his faith in Christ decrease significantly as the child grows older. When we read in Scripture that "a generation arose that knew not God" (Judges 2:10), we realize that parents must have dropped the baton.

Once the baton has been securely transferred to the next generation, the pressure remains. The parents must pray and cheer their child on as the child assumes the responsibility for getting the baton into the heart of the third generation. When their child finally passes that baton on and the parents watch their child walk in truth, they then experience the joy that comes from victory. *They can now rejoice!* One of the greatest joys of parenting comes from seeing their children walk in truth (3 John 4).

Truly, parents are primarily responsible for educating their children. Unfortunately, many of today's parents were not raised in homes where their parents successfully passed the baton of faith to them. However, this does not disqualify them from entering the race where they can become the first in line to pass the baton to their children. God expects parents to fulfill this responsibility by following His instructions on how to do it. Raising godly children must be the parents' goal and must be their highest priority in life.

Think About It

At the end of each chapter are a series of questions that are designed to help the reader internalize each principle of Kingdom Education™. These questions may be answered individually or in small group settings.

You may respond to the questions that best fits your role or you can answer questions in all of the sections. For example, parents should answer the questions in the parent section. However, parents can also attempt to answer the questions under the church and school sections in reference to the church and school they attend.

Restoring Individuals

Every individual Christian must develop a conviction that God has ordained parents to raise and educate their children. Therefore, parents have the primary responsibility to educate their children biblically. Each individual Christian needs to ask themselves the following questions.

1. What evidence is there that I believe that parents are primarily responsible for the education of their children?
2. How can I assist parents to understand and assume their God-given responsibility to provide their children with a biblically based education?

3. Does my life represent a lifestyle dedicated to advancing the home over other institutions that the world is advancing?
4. What am I doing to promote biblical family values versus the world's values?

Empowering Parents

Christian parents must make sure that they are assuming their God-given responsibility for the total education of their children. In doing so, parents must constantly ask themselves certain questions.

1. Who or what is in control of educating my child at home? What training is being done directly by me, the parent? What influence do I allow the media to have on my child at home? Do I know what my child is seeing, hearing, or doing while at home?
2. Do I know what my child is being taught in my neighborhood? What are other parents or peers teaching my child when they are together?
3. What is my child being taught in church, Sunday school, and other church-related activities?
4. What is my child learning at school? From teachers? From textbooks? From the curriculum? From other students? From the school's policies and procedures?

Engaging Churches

Churches must understand and support the fact that God first ordained the home and created within the home the necessary tools to educate their children biblically. Churches must challenge and equip parents to know and understand their parenting responsibilities as it was ordained by God at Creation.

1. Is the church conducting training for parents to actively fulfill their God-given responsibilities to educate their children biblically?
2. What evidences are there that the church believes that the parents have the primary responsibility for the education of their children?
3. Has the church attempted to replace the home in the equipping and preparing children for life and eternity?
4. How can the church raise up a generation of families who understand and are equipped to fulfill their responsibilities to educate their children biblically?

Transforming Schools

Christian schools exist to partner with the home; not replace it. Leaders, teachers, and staff must understand their role is to assist parents in providing a biblical education for their children. Educators need to ask themselves certain questions as they strive to support parents in this all-important task.

1. Is the school partnering with parents, or are parents required to partner with the school? What is the school doing to make sure that this is taking place?
2. How do the policies and practices of the school reinforce the principle that parents are primarily responsible for the education of their children?
3. How is the school helping and equipping parents to understand and embrace their God-given responsibility to provide their children with a biblically based education?
4. Are school activities scheduled in such a way that priority is given to families to have quality time with their children?

Chapter 2

The Scope of Education

Many people are dutiful churchgoers who remain otherwise spiritually inert because it is difficult to shape hearts and minds with only a few hours a week to work with.[11]

FAITH FOR EXILES

I HAVE FOUND OVER THE YEARS that when someone brings up the topic of education, it is usually seen in a very limited way. Everyone has heard the politician running for office talk about the importance of education. There has been an ongoing cry for educational reform in our country and the need to spend more and more money

---

11   David Kinnaman and Mark Matlock, *Faith for Exiles* (Grand Rapids: Baker Books, 2019) from a presentation Matlock gave at Rose Hill Christian School, Tomball, Texas (Feb. 26, 2020).

on education for as long as I can remember. There is no doubt that education is seen as an extremely important matter throughout society.

However, most references to education are merely about the *schooling* of children and youth. When education is equated only to schooling, its scope becomes very limited. This is why most people think that the education of children and youth begins at 8 a.m. and ends at 3 p.m. every Monday through Friday during the "school year." This is not what we find in Scripture when we try to understand the scope of education.

We just learned that the education of children and youth is the primary responsibility of parents. However, when does education begin and when does it end? This is the focus of the second biblical principle of Kingdom Education™.

Biblical Principle of Kingdom Education™ #2
The education of children and youth is a 24-hours-a-day, 7-days-a-week process that continues from birth till maturity.

> *You shall teach them diligently to your children, and shall talk of them when you sit in your house, when you walk by the way, when you lie down, and when you rise up.*
>
> *Deuteronomy 6:7*

> *You shall teach them to your children, speaking of them when you sit in your house, when you walk by the way, when you lie down, and when you rise up.*
>
> *Deuteronomy 11:19*

Train up a child in the way he should go: and when he is
old, he will not depart from it.

Proverbs 22:6

I am often invited to speak to a parent group or preach at a church about parenting and the education of children and youth. When such an opportunity presents itself, I begin by telling parents that they are responsible for the education their children receive. I explain how the education of children fits into God's priority list for parents.

Deuteronomy 6 is a key passage of Scripture for parents to study when they are trying to discern how important their homework assignments are in God's scheme of things. Deuteronomy is actually God's instructions to His people on how to obtain their inheritance from Him—the Promised Land.

For today's New Testament Christian, this book gives instructions on how to advance from new life in Christ to the abundant life in Christ that God has for His children. Deuteronomy 6 includes God's first set of instructions for obtaining this inheritance.

Here we find God telling His people that they must have a two-fold focus in their lives in order to be successful in living the abundant life. The first aspect of one's focus is found in verses 4 and 5.

Hear, O Israel: The Lord our God, the Lord is one! You
shall love the Lord your God with all your heart, with all
your soul, and with all your strength.

We are to love God with our entire being, all the time. Unfortunately, I have found myself, at times, loving my wife, my children, or my grandchildren more than I was loving God. I have even caught myself loving my *work for God* more than I was actually loving God.

The second aspect of one's focus is stated in verse 7.

> *You shall teach them diligently to your children…*

After focusing on God, we are to focus on the next generation. These two truths are so simple that we sometimes overlook them when it comes to how to educate our children and youth. We tend to make things more complicated than they really are in order to impress people. An example of this is found in a joke about the great detective, Sherlock Holmes.

One day Sherlock took his assistant, Watson, on a camping trip. They hiked deep into the woods, found an opening, and set up camp. That evening they made a fire, cooked some food, and ate dinner. As the evening went on, they went to sleep.

In the middle of the night, Sherlock woke Watson up and asked him to look up and tell him what he saw. Watson looked up into the dark night sky and told Sherlock that he saw the sky in a brilliant display of bright stars. Sherlock queried Watson, *What does that mean to you?*

In an effort to impress his boss, Watson thought about how to answer Sherlock. After a few seconds Watson said, *Astrologically, I see several constellations in the sky.* He thought a little more and said, *Astronomically, it tells me that there are billions of stars and hundreds of planets.*

Watson continued trying to impress his boss and said, *Theologically, the stars tell me that God is great and man is insignificant.* He continued trying to impress Sherlock with his wisdom and said, *Horologically, the stars indicate that it is around 3 a.m.* Finally, Watson said, *Meteorologically, the stars tell me that we are going to have good weather tomorrow.*

Watson was certain that he had impressed Sherlock by what it meant to look up into the sky and see billions of stars. So, Watson asked Sherlock, *What does it mean to you?*

After a moment of silence, Sherlock said, *Watson, you idiot, someone has stolen our tent!* In trying to impress his boss, Watson had missed the simple truth that the tent was gone.

The Christian life is simple and can be explained this way. As adults, Christians are to love God with all of their hearts, souls, and strength while they are here on earth. When they die, they go to Heaven where they will spend eternity with this great God.

However, they will all leave something behind them—the next generation. What does God want from the next generation? The same thing He wanted from them—to love Him completely.

However, God understands something that many Christian parents, church leaders and educators sometimes forget. The next generation won't love God this way by just being raised in a Christian home. Nor will it happen by going to church regularly. This will only happen when they are diligently taught the things of God.

I usually tell parents that there are only four times each day that God expects them to teach their children the things of God. When I make that statement, I can see many of them get something on which to write down or make note of what I am about to tell them. It is as if they are trying to find out the minimum that must be done in order to complete their homework assignments. I then proceed to tell them these four times.

- When they get up from bed (in the morning)
- Whenever they are in the house
- Whenever they are outside the house
- When they lie back down in bed (at night)

When I state these simple truths from Deuteronomy 6:7, there is a chuckle that is heard throughout the room. They realize that they are responsible for the education of their children all day long. Of course, I tell them the good news that it is not all day long. They don't have to do this while their children are asleep at night. Again, another chuckle is heard from the audience.

The simple "Sherlock" truth is that the education of our children is to be second in priority only to our love for God. This is what biblical discipleship is all about. It must be seen as a 24-hours-a-day, 7-days-a-week process that begins at birth and goes on until maturity is reached.

Proverbs 22:6 is familiar to almost every Christian.

> *Train up a child in the way he should go: and when he is old, he will not depart from it.*

The words "train up" present parents with an interesting concept. I read in Bible times about how a mother when ready to give birth to a child, would call a midwife to assist her with the birth. When the baby was out of the womb, the midwife would take the child and clean it up and then do something very interesting.

The midwife would dip her finger in some plum juice and put it in the newborn's mouth and rub the child's gums with her finger. The bittersweet sensation on the baby's palate caused the little one to suck— desiring more. Once the sucking began, the midwife would give the child to the mother who would then begin to nurse her baby. The midwife knew that the child needed to get to the point quickly to want more of what he/she was experiencing on his/her gums so that the child could get the nourishment he/she needed to survive.

Christian parents must create that same thirst and hunger for God by dedicating their child to the Lord as soon as they are born. Then when the hunger and thirst begins, it must continue throughout the child's education.

I can remember being invited to share these biblical principles of education with the leaders of a discipleship department at a Christian publishing company several years ago. As I explained this second principle to them, I told them that this principle was followed by Jesus as He discipled the 12 men He had under His tutelage.

When Jesus set out and chose 12 men to disciple, He didn't tell them to spend all day Sunday and Wednesday night with Him. He didn't tell them to take a series of Bible studies and then they would become His disciples. No, He called them to leave everything and follow Him 24 hours a day, 7 days a week until they were thoroughly trained.

When I shared this with this discipleship team, their consensus belief was that people cannot do that today. They have family, church, and job responsibilities. They can't just stop everything and spend all day with Jesus. At the time, my response was that if the home, church, and school was united together, the next generation could experience exactly what Jesus' disciples did—24/7 instruction in God's truth.

Christian parents must first realize that they are primarily responsible for the education of their children. Then, they must understand that education is not limited just to the formal schooling their children receive. Education is the combined effort of the home, church, and school to teach their children what they need to know. It is an all-day job that takes place every day from birth until the parents release them as young adults.

The remaining biblical principles of Kingdom Education™ will provide parents, church leaders, and educators guidance on how to satisfactorily obey these first two principles. As you continue your pursuit to understand Kingdom Education™, you will find that each of the biblical principles are closely related to each other.

Think About It

Restoring Individuals

Every Christian needs to understand that the education of children and youth is an all-day, all-year process that begins at birth and continues on until the child is a mature adult. In order to internalize this principle, individuals need to look at their own lives and make sure they realize that they are influencing others and educating themselves 24/7. Christians must realize that they can only educate others out of their overflow of their relationship with Christ.

1. How much time am I spending in God's Word each day?
2. How does my relationship with Christ help me educate others that I have influence over?

3. Do I see every interaction with others as an opportunity to further their education and relationship with the Lord? What specifically have I done recently in accomplishing this?

Empowering Parents

Christian parents must understand that the discipleship of their children and youth takes place throughout every day of their lives. It is a process that takes no vacations and never really ends. This requires parents to carefully answer certain questions related to this principle.

1. What evidences are there that you view the education of your children a 24/7/365 process?
2. Have you created an intentional discipleship plan for your children?
3. Are you intentional to guard what comes into your home that can influence the heart and mind of your children?
4. Is your home one where your children feel safe to ask tough questions about everyday life?
5. Are you fully engaged in the education your children receive whenever they are away from home?

Engaging Churches

Church leaders must understand that the discipleship process is a 24-hour, 7-day-a-week process that begins at birth and continues on through maturity. This means that Sunday and Wednesday night services will not suffice to counteract the influence of secular education that occurs throughout the week. Churches need to address some very important issues in order to fulfill its mission of making disciples of all nations.

1. How can the church provide biblically based education for children throughout the week?
2. Does the church offer resources and/or training to help parents develop an intentional discipleship plan for their children?
3. Is the church willing to seek God's direction in *expanding ministry to include schooling*? (This is very different from merely starting a Christian school.)

Transforming Schools

Christian school educators must understand that education does not begin at 8 a.m. and end at 3 p.m. on Monday through Friday. Grasping this principle will require the school to be more intentional in partnering with the home and the church in the education of children. The following questions need to be addressed.

1. What strategies and practices does the school need to develop and implement so that the education the students are receiving at school is consistent with that which is taught at home and church?
2. What is the school doing to help parents be engaged in their children's school work?
3. How does this principle impact the school's extracurricular activities such as athletics, fine arts productions, mission opportunities, etc.?

Setting the Right Goals

Since making disciples is the main task of the church, every church ought to be able to answer two questions: What is our plan for making disciples of Jesus? Is our plan working?[12]
DALLAS WILLARD

SETTING AND ACHIEVING GOALS are common topics when discussing personal and corporate success. You can search the internet and find literally hundreds of books on how to set and achieve goals. One title that I found fascinating when doing such a search was *The Magic Lamp: Goal Setting for People Who Hate Setting* Goals.

We have all heard quotes like these about the importance of setting goals.

---

12   Quoted in article by Ben Sternke, "How I Make Disciples: Character and Competency," www.bensterke.com, May 14, 2012.

Setting goals is the first step in turning the invisible into the visible.

If you fail to plan, you are planning to fail.

*Your dreams are only your dreams until you
write them down—then they are goals.*

Goals are the fuel in the furnace of achievement.

If you aim at nothing, you'll hit it every time.

It is true that if a person does not set goals, he/she will never be able to achieve much in life. But what are the goals that parents, church leaders, and educators should set when it comes to educating future generations?

If I were to ask each reader to stop right now and write down the top five goals you have for your children or students, what would they be? Maybe an even bigger question might be, can you accomplish them?

Every now and then, I have asked a parent a simple question. Do you want your child to have a good education? Of course, every parent is quick to respond, yes (I would be very concerned if a parent were to tell me, no, I want my child to have the worst education possible). Then I ask the question, "Why?"

By far, the most common response I have gotten is an indication of what most parents believe should be the major goals of education. Most parents that I have asked this question respond with something like this. *I want them to get into a good college. I want them to be prepared for college. I want them to be successful in life.* How would you answer this question?

When parents, church leaders, or educators give me these types of responses, I ask one final question. *Why?* Why do you want them to be prepared for college or to get into a good college? How parents answer this question, reveals how they really define and view education.

Parents and teachers who have these goals for the education of their children most often view education to be equated to schooling. I have started asking a series of questions when addressing a group of teachers or parents. I first ask them if they agree with me that education is future-focused and is preparing children for the future. I always get an affirmative response from the entire group. Then I ask:

1. What does preschool prepare young children for? The group quickly responds with kindergarten.
2. What does kindergarten prepare young children for? Again, the response is first grade or elementary school.
3. What does elementary school prepare children for? Unanimously, they tell me middle school.
4. What does middle school prepare children for? You guessed it. Everyone replies high school.
5. What does high school prepare young people for? The response is always college.

The reality is that most parents, church leaders, and educators view the ***purpose or goal of schooling is merely to prepare children and youth for more schooling***. Thus, education in the home, church, and school is aimed at this very same goal—prepare them for more schooling.

As I am writing this book, I have been engaged in the field of education for over 50 years. There has been one major topic that I have heard stressed every year I have been in teaching. Throughout my teaching career, I have heard that our educational system (schooling) is broken and is in dire need of reform.

I cannot count how many new trends and/or ways of doing schooling have been invented over the course of my years in education. However, it doesn't appear that any of these efforts to reform education has worked. A couple of years ago, I watched an interview that was being conducted with the late Dr. Neil Postman. Postman was a renowned educator and prolific writer.

The interviewer asked Dr. Postman why efforts to reform education had failed. Postman's answer was quite profound. He said, "Reform efforts have failed because we are asking the wrong questions. We are only asking 'engineering' questions." I thought about that for a minute and had to agree. Most efforts to reform education have focused on how we perform the task of education. They have been on methodology and how to improve instruction.

Postman then said something very insightful. He said that reform efforts will never be effective until we answer the most important question that no one is even asking. ***Why Schooling?*** Postman hit the nail on the head. What is the purpose and goals of education? This is critical to making sure we address the issue of education biblically.

This leads us to the third biblical principle of Kingdom Education™.

Biblical Principle of Kingdom Education™ #3
The education of children and youth must have as its primary goals the salvation and the discipleship of the next generation.

"Therefore, go and make disciples of all the nations, baptizing them in the name of the Father and of the Son and of the Holy Spirit, teaching them to observe all things that I have commanded you; and lo, I am with you always, even to the end of the age." Amen.

Matthew 28:19-20

"That the generation to come might know them, the children who would be born, that they may arise and declare them to their children, that they may set their hope in God, and not forget the works of God, but keep His commandments;"

Psalm 78:6-7

When I share this with Christian educators, I have been shocked to hear some of them tell me that salvation and discipleship are "church" activities. We are schools and our activities are all about "academics."

It is clear that they do not understand biblical discipleship. They see discipleship as going through a series of Bible studies and that is something that is the church's responsibility—not the school's. True discipleship is all about leading an individual to be a Christ follower, and that person's relationship with Jesus Christ must impact all of life.

Philip May, in his book *Which Way to Educate?*, compares today's educator [parent] to the field general who has become so involved in the details and strategies of the immediate battle that he has lost sight of the overall strategy of the war or has actually forgotten why it is being fought.[13] I have found this to be the case for many Christian parents, church leaders, and educators today. We are so entangled in the affairs of this world that we forget our ultimate purpose for being here. We

---

13   Philip May, *Which Way to Educate?* (Chicago, Moody Press: 1975), 9

are trying to survive in today's frantic, fast-paced culture and end up setting goals that are merely temporal in nature.

Christians must never forget that one of the goals for the education of future generations must be their salvation. If every one of our children and grandchildren were to earn doctorates, become leaders of Fortune 500 companies, and accumulate vast riches here on earth and die without knowing Christ as their personal savior, what value would their education have had?

Unfortunately, this is not the most important goal for many Christians when it comes to raising their children. The Barna Group did a study about parenting in 2005. Their findings were quite alarming. Only one out of every five parents (20%) mentioned having a significant faith commitment as an ingredient required for parental success.

When parents were asked to describe the most important outcomes, they were devoted to help their children experience, the top outcome was *getting a good education* (39%). Third in priority was having a meaningful relationship with Jesus Christ at only 22% which is only two out of every ten parents. Ten percent of parents merely wanted their children to be happy as their top priority in parenting.

One might expect that born-again parents would have different goals for their children. However, the study showed that there was very little difference when comparing unsaved and saved parents. Only 30% of born-again parents included the salvation of their child in the list of critical parental emphases.

Another alarming finding was that only 43% of parents surveyed said that they taught their children that there were "some" moral absolutes found in the Bible, and 45% said they taught there are no such absolutes.

Born-again parents were somewhat stronger in their parenting practices when it comes to teaching children about biblical moral absolutes. Still, less than six of ten Christian parents taught their children that the Bible contains absolute moral values.

Parents, church leaders, and educators must keep the Gospel central in the entire educational process. The salvation of the next generation must be first and foremost in our educational goals. The second major goal of education must be the discipleship of future generations.

I want to make a bold statement at this juncture. I am convinced that every child will be discipled! Discipleship is not an option. It is a fact of life. So, the question is not will our children be discipled, but who or what will disciple them?

The Gospel writer Luke made this point crystal clear.

> *A disciple is not above his teacher, but everyone who is perfectly trained will be like his teacher.*
> *Luke 6:40*

This leads me to another conviction that has a grip on me. All education is aimed at making future generations disciples of someone or something! Christians must grasp this truth and then apply it to their goals for the education of their children and youth.

When one sees the term "discipleship" in this principle, it refers to one becoming a disciple of Jesus Christ—not just a disciple of anyone or anything. Again, I want to emphasize the reality that every child will be discipled by someone or something. The education a child receives at home, school, and church will determine whose disciple he/she will be.

How can Christians assess whether or not they are being successful in reaching this all-important goal? To do this, we must look at the Great Commission in more detail. Jesus gave this instruction just before He ascended into Heaven. Allow me to repeat these words found in Matthew 28.

> *Therefore go and make disciples of all the nations, baptizing them in the name of the Father and of the Son and of the Holy Spirit, teaching them to observe all things that I have commanded you…*

Jesus is telling His disciples that they are to make disciples of all nations. Of course, evangelism is implied to be a part of this effort. I think that we would all agree that one must be born again in order to be able to become a disciple of Jesus Christ.

However, discipleship actually plays the biggest part of this commission. After a person becomes a Christian, the rest of Jesus' instruction is all about discipleship—teaching them to obey everything God commands them in Scripture.

From this understanding, one can assess the discipleship that is taking place with our children and youth. We can know who or what is discipling our children by observing whose commands they are obeying. Are they obeying God's Word, or are they obeying the culture or the world? This is the measure of discipleship, and it is determined by the education they receive at home, church, and school.

The reality is that the younger generations alive today are not being led to be disciples of Jesus Christ. Just the opposite is true. Study after study shows that the vast majority of young people that are in our homes and churches are leaving the faith. They have been discipled through a secular education and are following the ways of the world rather than Christ. The home, church, and school must reprioritize their goals for the education of their children and youth to be in line with God's Word.

Think About It

Restoring Individuals

The Bible teaches that it is important to have a vision for our lives. God's vision for each of us should be the driving force behind any goals that one sets in his/her life. We must be intentional in setting goals that are eternal in nature rather than simply setting goals that are temporal and self-centered. The following questions should guide us in setting right goals.

1. Am I seeking God's kingdom as my first priority in life? What are some evidences that I am doing this on a consistent basis?
2. What have you believed to be the main goals when it comes to the education of children?
3. Are my current goals for my life temporal or eternal in nature? What, if any, changes do I need to make in my goal setting that will cause me to seek what is eternal and not temporal?

Empowering Parents

Every parent wants to see his/her child succeed. Parents go to great lengths to see their child achieve certain things in life. Parents need to make sure that the goals they have for their children have an eternal focus. The following questions need to be answered in order to ensure that the education parents give their children will help them reach the most important goals in life that are presented in this principle.

1. How would answer this question? Do you want your children to have a good education?
2. Why do you want your children to have a good education?
3. Were your answers to these two questions focused on the temporal or the eternal?
4. What is the ultimate goal for which each child has been created?
5. Is the education I provide for my child focused on his/her salvation and becoming a dedicated follower of Jesus Christ? Give evidence that this is true.

Engaging Churches

Churches talk a lot about evangelism and discipleship. Church leaders should always place the highest priority on seeing every person coming to know Christ as his/her Lord and Savior. However, the Great Commission tasks the church to make disciples of every nation. Evangelism is the first step in making a disciple, but the process does not stop with salvation. Certain questions need to be addressed for the church to fulfill its mission that Jesus gave in Matthew 28.

1. What is the church doing to make sure every child hears the Gospel and has the opportunity to come to Christ?
2. What is the church doing to help parents understand that the salvation of their children must be their highest priority and receive their greatest attention and effort?
3. Does the church see the education of children and youth as a discipleship process?
4. How is the church following Jesus' example of discipleship? Jesus did not have the 12 men meet with him on Sundays and Wednesday nights for Bible studies. He spent every day, all day with them for three full years. What can the church do to make

disciples of its children and youth? What would that look like in partnering with the home? What would that look like when it comes to their schooling?

Transforming Schools

Some educators have falsely claimed that evangelism and discipleship are functions of the church. Schools are all about academics. The Gospel must be at the center of every Christian school, and the educational process must be seen as the making of disciples of Jesus Christ. This requires educators to answer some very important questions.

1. Does the school keep the Gospel central in all that it does? How is this done? Is every teacher able to lead a student to a saving knowledge of Jesus Christ?
2. How is the school discipling its students that have a personal relationship with Jesus?
3. Since discipleship is an all-day, all-week process, how does the school connect with the home and local churches to be more effective in making disciples of its students?
4. What does the school do to equip its faculty and staff to disciple their students?
5. What can the school start doing to make sure that the salvation and discipleship of its students are the two most important goals in the school's educational programs?

Chapter 4

The Importance of Truth

Bible reading is an education in itself.[14]
LORD TENNYSON

SINCE THE BEGINNING OF TIME, humans have had a love-hate relationship with the truth. We have sought truth. Abandoned truth. Debated truth. And most recently been provided with a global system that allows us to create, deliver, and share our own versions of the truth with the world. Sometimes, we find ourselves hiding from the truth, while other times, we discover ourselves running from the consequences that the truth brings to light.

Somehow, deep inside, humans realize that without truth, it is impossible to find meaning because ultimately everything becomes something

---

14   Alfred Lord Tennyson, *AZQuotes.com* (Wind and Fly LTD, 2021), https://www.azquotes.com/quote/543324, accessed 2021.

that could be a lie. The war that rages in our own hearts can be seen throughout our culture as well. Our generation even has created a phrase to describe it. False news.

It is this battle to discern the truth that can be traced through every generation all the way back to Genesis chapter three when the enemy of God invited Eve to doubt the words of God. That initial attack on the Word of God leads us to our fourth principle.

Biblical Principle of Kingdom Education™ #4
The education of children and youth must be based on God's Word as absolute truth.

> *Heaven and earth will pass away, but My words will by no means pass away.*
>
> *Matthew 24:35*

> *Forever, O Lord, Your word is settled in heaven.*
> *Psalm 119:89*

> *The grass withers, the flower fades, but the word of our God stands forever.*
>
> *Isaiah 40:8*

Ultimately, culture wars are fought over two fundamental questions.

1. What is reality?
2. What is truth?

While some argue for objective truth, others hold to the belief that truth is subjective. The truth is that ultimately the answer is that truth is neither. In John 14:6, Jesus declared that He is the truth. Truth is neither objective nor is it subjective. It is personified. Jesus is truth. Truth is not something that God simply decided and then forced upon us. At its very essence, nor is it a characteristic of God. It is the very nature of God.

Watch how the Apostle John introduces us to this reality in the introduction to the Gospel that bears his name.

> *In the beginning was the Word, and the Word was with God, and the Word was God. The same was in the beginning with God. All things were made by Him; and without Him was not anything made that was made. In Him was life; and the life was the light of men…And the Word was made flesh, and dwelt among us, and we beheld His glory, the glory as of the only begotten of the Father, full of grace and truth.*
>
> *John 1:1-4,14*

From this passage of Scripture, we learn that Jesus Christ and the Word are one. Combining the fact that John 14:6 tells us that Jesus is the Truth with the fact that Jesus and the Word are one, we can state with confidence that the Word is Truth. The Bible is the eternal, inerrant, infallible, and sufficient Word of God.

When we are considering how God wants us to educate future generations, we must fully embrace the fact that God's Word is the only source of absolute truth. In today's world, there is a denial of the reality that there is absolute truth. In fact, a recent study showed that up to 69% of the Millennial generation no longer accepts the possibility that there is absolute truth.

We have to understand that God's Word must be the foundation that undergirds all learning. Whenever God's Word is removed from any facet of education, that education becomes mere human indoctrination. Such education always evolves into empty philosophies that deceive and take one captive by following human tradition and the basic principles of this world (Colossians 2:8).

Any education that is not based on God's Word as absolute truth is a myth. Kingdom Education™ is based on the Word of God; therefore, true education must be Bible-based.

Benjamin Rush was one of the Founding Fathers of the United States. He was one of the most prolific writers among this group of men. He was very concerned about what the consequences would be if the Bible were removed from the education of the youth. He wrote,

> *In contemplating the political institutions of the United States, [if we were to remove the Bible from schools] I lament that we waste so much time and money in punishing crimes and take so little pains to prevent them. We profess to be republicans, and yet we neglect the only means of establishing and perpetuating our republic forms of government, that is, the universal education of our youth in the principles of Christianity by means of the Bible.*[15]

Rush went on to state his belief that:

> *No man was ever early instructed in the truths of the Bible without having been made wiser or better by the early operation of these impressions upon his mind.*[16]

---

15   Benjamin Rush, *Essays, Literary, Moral and Philosophical* (Philadelphia: Thomas and William Bradford, 1806), 113.

16   Rush, The Bible in Schools (Garland, TX: The American Tract Society, 1995), quoted in "The Great Worth of the Bible in School," Christian School Comment 26, no. 8 (Colorado Springs: ACSI, 1995).

God's Word must be the cornerstone of the entire educational process that Christians provide for their children and youth. Dr. Roy Lowrie, Jr., had a profound influence on my life and how I view education. I can well remember sitting under his instruction as he instilled in us how God's Word must be the filter by which all knowledge is interpreted.

He did this by holding up two books—the Bible and a book written by a person. He would explain to us that there are three ways of comparing the two books. One way was to hold the Bible and man's book side by side. In this way, we can pull what we like from both sources and determine what is true.

The second way that Lowrie said we could compare the two pieces was to hold man's book between our eyes and the Bible. By doing this, we would interpret what the Bible says through the lens of the book that man had written.

The final and correct way to interpret any knowledge is to hold the Bible in between anything that man has written and our eyes. This way we interpret all of man's writings through the lens of God's absolute truth.

Pastor and author, Kevin Swanson, wrote related to the importance of God's Word in the education of our children and youth. He wrote:

> *The content of education must be literally bathed in God's Word...God's Word is to be, literally 'in their faces'...they [our children] should never get the impression that the Word is something they run into in some religious ritual on Sunday while the rest of their education, entertainment, family time, and so forth is completely void of the Word or even opposed to it.*[17]

17 Kevin Swanson, *Upgrade: 10 Secrets to the best Education for Your Child* (Nashville: B&H Publishers, 2010), 170.

This concept of making sure that the Bible is "in our children's faces" during the entire educational process is not something Swanson or anyone else simply came up with. No, it is taken directly from God's Word.

> *You shall bind them as a sign on your hand, and they shall*
> *be as frontlets between your eyes. You shall write them on*
> *the doorposts of your house and on your gates.*
>
> Deuteronomy 6:8-9

When you read these two verses in their context, you quickly will understand that it is God's Word, His Truth that must be in front of our children and youth throughout their daily lives. This is especially true for their education.

When the Bible is not viewed as being the only source of absolute truth and is not the foundation of the education our children receive, the consequences are devastating. Theologians throughout the history of the New Testament church understood this and sounded strong warnings concerning the importance of God's Word in the educational process.

> *Withdraw from a child the only divine rule of life, and the*
> *result will be most lamentable. An education purely secular*
> *is the handmaiden of godless skeptics.*[18]
>
> C. H. Spurgeon

> *I advise no one to place his child where the Scriptures*
> *do not reign paramount. Every institution that does*

---

18   Quoted by William F. Stevens in the article "A Shelter in a Time of Storm," *Christian Educators Journal* 32, no. 4 (April 1993), 10.

not unceasingly pursue the study of god's Word becomes corrupt.[19]

Martin Luther

The Bible IS the authority, the final resting place of our cares, our worries, our griefs, our tragedies, our sorrows and our surprises. It is the final answer to our questions, our search. Turning back to the Scriptures will provide that nothing else on the entire earth can provide.[20]

Charles Swindoll

Kingdom Education™ requires that God's Word is "in our face!"

Think About It

Restoring Individuals

Every Christian must seek to find and know truth. Today's culture says that absolute truth does not exist and, therefore, one must simply know his/her truth. For the Christian, there is absolute truth and it is found in God's Word. Because of this fact, every Christian must base everything in life on the truth of God's Word. The following questions are important to finding truth.

1. Do you believe that there is absolute truth that is true for every person regardless of culture?

---

19 Martin Luther, *AZQuotes.com* (Wind and Fly LTD, 2021), https://www.azquotes.com/quote/526176, accessed 2021.

20 Charles Swindoll, *Growing Deep in the Christian Life* (Portland, OR: Multnomah Press, 1986), 56.

2. How much time do you spend reading, studying, memorizing, and meditating on God's Word?
3. Is the Bible something that you merely bump into on Sundays, while the rest of the week, it sits idle on a table?
4. Can you apply God's Word to every aspect of your life: i.e., social life, work, marriage, parenting, government/politics, etc.?

Empowering Parents

Every Christian home must be built on the foundation of God's Word. The Bible must be the defining point of all knowledge taught to one's children. Parents cannot fulfill their God-given responsibilities of raising their children apart for God's Word. This requires parents to constantly ask themselves the following questions.

1. Does the authority of Scripture guide your decisions at home?
2. Do your children see you spending time in the Word throughout the week?
3. Do your children hear you refer to Scripture as you make everyday decisions?
4. Do your children know that you believe that God's Word is absolute truth?
5. Are you allowing your children to be educated in a way that denies the existence of absolute truth and/or discredits the Bible?

Engaging Churches

The church is the God-ordained institution to advance His kingdom throughout a lost and dark world. The Bible must be held as the only source of absolute truth if the church is going to fulfill its mission.

This applies to the church's role in educating future generations. This requires church leaders to respond to some very important questions.

1. Does the church preach and teach the whole counsel of God as presented in the Holy Scriptures?
2. Does the church teach that the Bible is the inerrant and sufficient Word of God?
3. Is the Bible the primary source for all teaching and preaching that takes place at the church?
4. Does the church stress to its members that they must be reading and studying God's Word each and every day? What evidence does the average church attendee see while at church that would cause them to make this a priority at home?
5. How does the church help parents and teachers place God's Word as the foundation of the education children and youth receive at home, church, and school?

Transforming Schools

The school must help all students understand that there is absolute, objective truth that applies to every person, no matter where they live. This requires that the Bible has precedent over anything that people may write and/or produce. Several questions must be addressed to ensure that God's Word is seen as absolute truth and is the foundation of all knowledge found in every subject that is taught.

1. What evidences are there that shows that the Bible is foundational to the entire educational program at the school? Is it studied in staff devotions? If so, how often? Is it an often referred to source in staff meetings and professional development?

2. How is God's Word, the Bible, integrated into the school's entire program?

3. Are teachers required to earn CEUs or other types of credit in actual Bible studies?

4. What is the school's policy when a textbook, program, outside speaker, etc., does not align itself with Scripture?

5. What role do students see the Bible plays in all their subjects, activities, fine arts productions, and athletics?

Chapter 5

The Center of Everything

Christ is Himself the eternal God, the ultimate source of all truth and of our capacity for knowing anything at all.
ARTHUR F. JONES

EVERY PERSON PUTS SOMETHING or someone at the center of his/her life. We do this because we are looking for something that will give us ultimate satisfaction, happiness, and joy. Whatever is placed at the center of one's life is what that person worships. It is the person's true god.

Pastor and author, Tim Keller, says this about the necessity for people to worship something.

> *Either you worship God or you will be worshipping something else—there is not the alternative of not*

worshipping. Either you will be looking to God for your significance and security or you will be looking to something else (even if it is your own abilities).[21]

How do you change behavior? Change what you worship.[22]

Nancy Pearcey, in her book, *Finding Truth*, says that *God cannot be rejected without putting something else in its place.*[23] A person will worship God or will try and substitute something else in God's creation to worship. A. W. Tozer explains how man was created by God to worship Him.

God made us to worship Him, and if we had not fallen with Adam and Eve, worship [of God] would have been the most natural thing for us.[24]

We were created to worship, so we must find someone or something to be at the center of our lives in order to fulfill this God-given drive. This is true for the education we give our children and youth. There is some god that we pursue and worship driving all of our educational efforts. This leads us to the fifth principle of Kingdom Education™.

---

21   Tim Keller (@DailyKeller), Twitter, June 12, 2019

22   Tim Keller (@DailyKeller), Twitter, May 3, 2019.

23   Nancy Pearcey, *Total Truth: Liberating Christianity from Its Cultural Captivity* (Wheaton, IL: Crossway Books, 2004), 23, 41.

24   Morning and Evening with A.W. Tozer, November 27th, Evening, "Humans Judge the Lord?". https://www.studylight.org/daily-devotionals/eng/toz.html?date=11/27._

Biblical Principle of Kingdom Education™ #5

The education of children and youth must hold Christ preeminent in all of life.

...in whom [Jesus] are hidden all the treasures of wisdom and knowledge.

Colossians 2:3

Woe to you lawyers! For you have taken away the key of knowledge. You did not enter in yourselves, and those who were entering in you hindered.

Luke 11:52

As you therefore have received Christ Jesus the Lord, so walk in Him, rooted and built up in Him and established in the faith, as you have been taught, abounding in it with thanksgiving. Beware lest anyone cheat you through philosophy and empty deceit, according to the tradition of men, according to the basic principles of the world, and not according to Christ. For in Him dwells all the fullness of the Godhead bodily; and you are complete in Him, who is the head of all principality and power.

Colossians 2:6-10

He [Jesus] is the image of the invisible God, the firstborn over all creation. For by Him all things were created that are in heaven and that are on earth, visible and invisible, whether thrones or dominions or principalities or powers. All things were created through Him and for Him. And He is before all things, and in Him all things consist. And He is the head of the body, the church, who is the beginning, the

*firstborn from the dead, that in all things He may have
the preeminence.*

Colossians 1:15-18

*… that at the name of Jesus every knee should bow, of
those in heaven, and of those on earth, and of those under
the earth, and that every tongue should confess that Jesus
Christ is Lord, to the glory of God the Father.*

Philippians 2:10-11

The entire educational process must be biblical and Christ-centered.
We see from the verses above that in Christ are "hid all the treasures
of wisdom and knowledge." This means that He must be central to all
that takes place as we educate our children and youth. This applies to
the home, church, and school.

When Jesus Christ is removed from any aspect of a child's education,
dire consequences result. In Jesus' day, the lawyers were the teachers of
the day. In Luke, Jesus condemns the lawyers because they had removed
the "key of knowledge" from their teaching. This key refers to Jesus. The
results were disastrous. First, these teachers couldn't enter into God's
kingdom. Second, and even more consequential, was the fact that those
who were entering into the kingdom were being hindered from doing
so (Luke 11:52). When Christ is not central to the education of our
children, they will be hindered from learning truth.

Why does Scripture demand that Jesus Christ be preeminent in
everything? I believe that it is because of not only who Jesus is but also
what Jesus did. We already know that Jesus is the Son of God. He is
the Word. He is the Truth. He is everything. Knowing this about who
Jesus is demands that He has preeminence.

However, when one considers what Jesus did, the need for Him to have center stage in every aspect of life becomes crystal clear. Consider this passage of Scripture.

> *Let this mind be in you which was also in Christ Jesus, who, being in the form of God, did not consider it robbery to be equal with God, but made Himself of no reputation, taking the form of a bondservant, and coming in the likeness of men. And being found in appearance as a man, He humbled Himself and became obedient to the point of death, even the death of the cross.*
>
> *Philippians 2:5-8*

Because of the sacrifice Christ made on the cross on behalf of all men and in humble obedience to His Father, His name has been exalted above all other names (Philippians 2:5-11). He became my sin and paid the price for it. Because of this sacrifice, God declares that Jesus is to be preeminent in everything—period. This means that the education children receive at home, church, and school must hold Christ preeminent in the entire process.

John Milton understood this in the 1600s when he wrote,

> *The end then of learning is to repair the ruins of our first parents by regaining to know God aright, and out of that knowledge to love Him, to imitate Him, to be like Him.*[25]

---

25 John Milton, Of Education, in *Basic Writings in Christian Education*, ed. Kendig Brubaker Cully (Philadelphia: The Westminster Press, 1960), 24.

Think About It

Restoring Individuals

Every person is created for one purpose, to bring glory to God in everything we say, think, and do. In order for us to do this, we must make Jesus Christ preeminent in all of life, including the education of future generations. This leads us to consider some very important questions.

1. What evidences do you have that demonstrates that Jesus Christ is central to your very being? What do others see in you that causes them to see Christ?
2. What areas of your life are not under the Lordship of Christ?
3. What temptations do I face that cause me to focus on things of this world and not on Christ?
4. Have I been taken captive by deceptive, worldly philosophies rather than by Christ (see Colossians 2:8)?

Empowering Parents

God wants our homes to be places where Jesus Christ has the preeminence. Jesus desires to be Lord of all which means our homes must make Him our central focus. This means that He must be the main focus in the education we give our children. Some of the questions we need to answer will prove whether or not Jesus Christ is preeminent in our homes.

1. Is my home a place where we can truly say, Jesus above all? What are some specific evidences that our children will see that this is true?

2. Does Jesus Christ rule in our relationships in our family? Is there Christlike love lived out in everyday life?
3. Is Jesus Christ preeminent in the education my children receive at home? In their school? In their church? Give specific examples that proves this to be true in each place.

Engaging Churches

Jesus Christ is the head of the church. This is evidenced by the church submitting to Him in every area of ministry. Church leaders need to hold Christ preeminent and obey Him, especially in the education of future generations. How would you answer these questions?

1. What evidences will people see that Jesus Christ is central to every ministry of the church?
2. What does the church do to ensure that all of its ministries are not personality driven but Word driven?
3. What is and what can the church do to help parents provide their children with an education that holds Jesus Christ preeminent?

Transforming Schools

Colossians 1:9 states that Jesus Christ is to have the preeminence in all things. This means that He must be the main focus in all the school does. The phrase, *it is all about Jesus*, should be the driving force behind the entire educational program of the school. Consider the following questions.

1. How does the school put Jesus Christ at its center? Give specific ways that the school ensures that this is a reality in all it does.

2. What strategies does the school employ to help the faculty and staff keep Christ first in their lives and their teaching?

3. If someone visits the school's website or reads the school's promotional material, what will he/she think is of highest priority at the school?

4. What can the school do to exalt Jesus Christ above everything else?

Chapter 6

Millstones, Anyone?

To harm one of "these little ones" was
to court the judgement of God.[26]
ARCHBISHOP HARRY GOODHEW

WHILE JESUS WAS HERE ON EARTH, He had a deep concern for the wellbeing of children. In one instance, parents wanted to have Jesus bless their children. When they heard that Jesus was in the area, they went out to see Him with their children at their side.

When Jesus' disciples saw parents bringing their children to where Jesus was teaching and healing people, they became indignant. They told the parents to take their children home. The Master was too busy to be

---

26 Archbishop Harry Goodhew, "41. 'Lead A Child Astray? You'd Be Better Off Drowned!' – Jesus," *WhatDidJesusSay.com*, https://whatdidjesussay.com/41-lead-a-child-astray-youd-be-better-off-drowned-jesus/.

bothered with these little ones running all over the place and creating distractions.

Jesus strongly rebuked His disciples for their actions. Then Jesus said something very profound. He told His disciples to *let the little children come to Me, and do not forbid them; for such is the kingdom of heaven (Matthew 18:6).* This was an unprecedented position to take in those days. Children were not seen as having any significant value.

Jesus was always concerned for the safety and protection of young children. He knew that the enemy had his sights set on taking these little ones captive to his desires. The sixth principle of Kingdom Education™ deals with how Jesus demands that children are to be protected.

Biblical Principle of Kingdom Education™ #6
The education of children and youth must not hinder the spiritual and moral development of the next generation.

> *But whoever causes one of these little ones who believe in Me to sin, it would be better for him if a millstone were hung around his neck, and he were drowned in the depth of the sea.*
>
> *Matthew 18:6*

> *Then little children were brought to Him that He might put His hands on them and pray, but the disciples rebuked them. But Jesus said, "Let the little children come to Me, and do not forbid them; for of such is the kingdom of heaven."*
>
> *Matthew 19:13*

Then they brought little children to Him, that He might touch them; but the disciples rebuked those who brought them. But when Jesus saw it, He was greatly displeased and said to them, "Let the little children come to Me, and do not forbid them; for of such is the kingdom of God. Assuredly, I say to you, whoever does not receive the kingdom of God as a little child will by no means enter it." And He took them up in His arms, laid His hands on them, and blessed them.

Mark 10:13-16

Then they also brought infants to Him that He might touch them; but when the disciples saw it, they rebuked them. But Jesus called them to Him and said, "Let the little children come to Me, and do not forbid them; for of such is the kingdom of God. Assuredly, I say to you, whoever does not receive the kingdom of God as a little child will by no means enter it."

Luke 18:15-17

Jesus showed a special love for children throughout His earthly ministry. When the disciples tried to keep children from getting too close to Jesus, He rebuked them very firmly. This account is recorded in three of the four gospels. So, we know children are of utmost importance to Him.

Why would Jesus want children to come close to Him? We must remember who Jesus said He was while He was here on earth. He declared, *I am the resurrection and the life, the way, the truth and the life, living water, the bread of life, the good shepherd—I am everything! Why would you want to keep children from me?*

It was in this context that Jesus made statements about the seriousness of offending a young person as noted in Matthew 18 above. Sometimes, we think of offending children only in terms of physical abuse, neglect, or molestation. However, Scripture makes it clear that anything that might hinder a child's moral and spiritual development is the epitome of child abuse.

When false teachers creep into the church, there is usually an outrage that rises up against it. This is especially true when it takes place in the youth and/or children's ministries. God's Word warns Christians how they must be vigilant for wolves in sheep's clothing creeping into the church.

However, Christians don't consistently apply these warnings to the education that takes place in the home and the school. Let me share a personal example of how this principle showed up in my home several years ago.

The family was all together watching a program on TV. As we were watching, I felt the Lord asking me some questions. The questions went like this.

1. Do you see these children as my homework assignments to you and your wife? My answer was yes.
2. Are you following my directions on how to educate these children as you try to complete your assignment? Again, I answered that I am trying to obey them.
3. Is the program you are watching drawing your children closer to Jesus or pushing them away? I hesitated to answer this question.

I had never thought of this principle applying to what we were watching on television. Now I realize that education is not merely what takes place in a school. It also takes place in the home and church 24 hours per day, 7 days per week.

The problem that so many Christians face, when it comes to following principles like this, is the fact that many Christians have developed a dualistic worldview. Dualism occurs when one divides his/her life into two compartments—the secular and the sacred.

By doing this, Christians try to live the sacred part of their lives from a biblical perspective. At the same time, they apply a secular worldview to the secular areas of their lives. This results in people's lives being very fragmented with no congruent sense of purpose.

Many Christians would be quick to deny evolution, communism, and gender fluidity teaching to take place in their homes and churches. At the same time, they continue to let these false philosophies and ideas be taught to their children at school.

This biblical principle must be applied to the entire educational process that children and youth are involved in. When it is consistently applied, we realize that we must evaluate everything that takes place in our homes, churches, and schools. Are there things that are being taught to our children that go against the truths of God's Word? Are they sitting under teaching that draws them closer to God or drives them away?

We cannot afford to allow any aspect of our children's education to hinder their moral and spiritual development. If we fail in applying this principle consistently to the entire educational process, do we deserve some millstones?

Think About It

Restoring Individuals

Every child is very special to the Lord. Therefore, it is of utmost importance that every Christian protect a child from harm. We must not only protect them from physical harm but also from emotional, mental, and spiritual harm. That is why Christians must address some fundamental questions when it comes to the protection of children and youth.

1. Are there sinful habits in your life that would harm a child if he/she would follow your example? What do I need to do to break these habits?
2. What are you doing to protect children and youth that you have influence over from dangerous philosophies and practices?
3. Have you developed the ability to discern things in this world that are dangerous to one's physical, emotional, mental, and spiritual life?

Empowering Parents

Parents are the primary caregivers of their children. They, more than anyone else, are responsible for their protection from anything that will harm them. This responsibility requires parents to continually give their attention to several important questions.

1. What are some ways you protect your children physically?
2. What are you doing to protect your children emotionally and mentally?

3. How are you protecting your children from spiritual or moral harm?

4. Is there anything that needs to change in your home to better protect your children spiritually and morally?

5. Does the education your children receive at church and school protect their hearts and minds from dangerous secular philosophies? What about the textbooks and resources that they are using? Do they present dangerous anti-Christian philosophies and worldviews?

Engaging Churches

The Scriptures are filled with warnings to the church to guard against false teachers and teachings. This is because this will bring spiritual and moral harm to the church's members. It is even more critical to ensure that the children and youth are protected from false ideas and philosophies. In order to guard the church doors from these vices, it is necessary to address some key questions.

1. Is the church teaching and preaching the Word of God as absolute truth?

2. Does the church host or support activities that can hinder the spiritual and moral development of children and youth?

3. What is the church doing to make sure that every teacher and lesson is grounded in the truth of God's Word?

4. How is the church protecting children and youth from spiritual and moral harm when it comes to their education in the church, at home, and at school?

Transforming Schools

Everything that a school does impacts its students morally and spiritually. This is because there is no such thing as spiritually neutral education. Schools must be intentional in making sure that nothing takes place at the school that hinders the student's spiritual and moral development.

1. Are there programs and/or activities at the school that operate in opposition to God's Word, especially in the areas of biblical morality?
2. What does the school do to make sure that all staff members hold true to biblical standards of morality in their personal lives and in their teaching and interaction with students?
3. What can the school do to strengthen their staff members so that they will build students up in Christ and not lead them away from Him?
4. What is the school doing to make sure a biblical worldview is at the heart of every class, activity, program, and policy of the school?
5. How does the school protect students spiritually and morally from false philosophies found in textbooks and other teaching resources?
6. How does the school partner with the home and church to not only protect children from harmful things but also prepare students to be able to discern spiritually harmful philosophies?

Chapter 7

Help Me!

Whoever spends one second with a child's mind needs to have a biblical worldview.[27]
DR. LARRY TAYLOR

EDUCATING CHILDREN IS an overwhelming responsibility for parents to faithfully fulfill. Trying to balance work and family life is difficult enough. When one adds to these tasks the education of our children and youth, it can seem impossible to handle.

What is a parent to do? How can they get help with this enormous undertaking? The answer to these questions is found in the seventh principle of Kingdom Education™.

---

27 Dr. Larry Taylor, Zoom interview as the new ACSI President.

Biblical Principle of Kingdom Education™ #7

The education of children and youth, if and when delegated to others by parents, must be done by teachers chosen with utmost care to ensure that they all follow these principles.

Moreover you shall select from all the people able men, such as fear God, men of truth, hating covetousness; and place such over them to be rulers of thousands, rulers of hundreds, rulers of fifties, and rulers of tens.

Exodus 18:21

For this child I prayed, and the Lord has granted me my petition which I asked of Him. Therefore I also have lent him to the Lord; as long as he lives he shall be lent to the Lord." So they worshiped the Lord there.

1 Samuel 1:27-28

Now the boy Samuel ministered to the Lord before Eli. And the word of the Lord was rare in those days; there was no widespread revelation. And it came to pass at that time, while Eli was lying down in his place, and when his eyes had begun to grow so dim that he could not see, and before the lamp of God went out in the tabernacle of the Lord where the ark of God was, and while Samuel was lying down, that the Lord called Samuel. And he answered, "Here I am!" So he ran to Eli and said, "Here I am, for you called me." And he said, "I did not call; lie down again." And he went and lay down. Then the Lord called yet again, "Samuel! So Samuel arose and went to Eli, and said, "Here I am, for you called me." He answered, "I did not call, my son; lie down again." (Now Samuel did not yet know the Lord, nor was the word of the Lord yet revealed to him.) And the Lord called Samuel again the third time. So he arose and went to Eli, and said, "Here I am, for you did call me. Then Eli perceived that the Lord had called the boy. Therefore Eli said to Samuel, "Go, lie down; and it shall be, if He calls you, that you must say, 'Speak, Lord, for Your servant hears.' " So Samuel went and lay down in his place. Now the Lord came and stood and called as at other times, "Samuel! Samuel! And Samuel answered, "Speak, for Your servant hears."

1 Samuel 3:1-10

The task of raising children is awesome. It is becoming more demanding with each passing day. Every parent will in some way delegate some of this responsibility in the process of properly educating his/her children. This happens when we take them to church, allow them to go on the internet, or send them to school. This principle tells us that when parents need help, it is important that they take special care in choosing who will help them in this task.

Using the analogy that children are a homework assignment given to parents by God, we can look at the assignment that God gave to Moses to learn how to get the right help. Moses found himself overwhelmed with the task that God had given him. Moses was chosen by God to lead the Israelites out of Egypt and into the Promised Land. I don't know the exact number of Israelites that took this trip. But, I can say it was an extremely large number.

Moses was not only the leader of the nation, but he was also the teacher for all the people. I have often told teachers not to complain about the size of their classes. They could always have a class of hundreds of thousands of students like Moses had.

One day, Moses invited his father-in-law, Jethro, to accompany him as he went out to complete his assignment. We find this account in Exodus 18. Moses went out and judged the people. In other words, he taught them what was right and wrong from God's perspective. On this particular day, the Bible records that Moses judged or taught the people from morning until evening. No one can say that Moses worked "banker hours."

At the end of the day, Jethro asked Moses why he was the only one judging and teaching the entire nation. Moses responded that the people came to him because he alone knew the things of God. They had been in bondage for years and did not know God or His Word. So, Moses was tasked to "make known the statues of God and his laws."

Jethro spoke up and told Moses that what he was doing was good, but it would soon kill him. It was too much for one man to do. Added to all he had to do, think about the emotional and physical toll this task must have taken on Moses' life. Jethro explained that the task is too heavy or great for only one person to tackle. Moses needed help.

It was at this point that Jethro gave Moses a plan for getting the help he needed. Moses had to delegate some of his duties to other people. Moses would still be responsible for the entire nation, but others would help do some of the grunt work.

There have been books written on the importance of delegating and how to do it. In these books, one will find how many people should report to one person, how to organize a large group and break it into smaller ones. It seems like everyone knows and understands the need to delegate and how to do it.

However, Christians often overlook a very important aspect of effective delegation. The key to successfully delegating one's responsibilities to others is not found in how many people should report to an individual. The key ingredient to effective delegation involves who is chosen to help with any assignment.

Jethro told Moses that he should still be the people's representative before God. He should continue teaching the people the statues and laws and instructing them how to walk and work in line with God's will.

In addition to doing the assignment God had given him, Moses was told that he should select certain people to whom he could delegate some of his tasks. Here is the key to good delegation. Moses was to only choose "able" men. Notice it does not say that he should just choose anyone to help him.

God's Word goes on to define what makes up "able" men. In Exodus 18:21, we find God's definition of an "able" man.

> *you shall select from all the people able men, such as **fear God**, men **of truth**, **hating covetousness**; and place such over them to be rulers …*

There were three qualifications that a person had to possess in order to be chosen by Moses to assist him in his God-given assignment. Each person had to fear God. This is so important when one decides who is going to help parents educate their children. Christians should only choose men and women who fear God.

The second qualification is that these men had to love truth. We must remember that truth is a person—Jesus Christ. We have also seen that God's Word is truth since the Word and Jesus are one and the same. This means that those people that parents choose to help them educate their children must love God's Word.

Finally, the person must hate covetousness. Parents cannot afford to delegate any aspect of their God-given assignment to biblically educate their children to people who are in it just for the money.

There is no question that every parent will, at one time or another, have to delegate some of the tasks involved in educating his or her children to other people. When they do so, they should only choose men and women who fear God, love truth, and hate covetousness. Since Kingdom Education™ can only take place when God reigns in the entire educational process, it means that any teachers chosen to help parents with this assignment must follow these same biblical principles. Parents must choose able men and women to help them.

Think About It

Restoring Individuals

The key ingredient to effective delegation involves who is chosen to help with any assignment. Every individual has the ability to influence others in a way that builds them up in Christ or leads them away from Him. The following questions need to be addressed so that we are able and available to assist parents in biblically educating their children.

1. Would you be considered a person who fears God, loves truth and hates covetousness?
2. Do you understand that everything you say and do matters, especially when it comes to educating children and youth?
3. Are you currently in a position of influence on other people's children and youth? Will that influence cause others to love and fear God?
4. What evidences are there that you fear God and love truth?

Empowering Parents

Parents must understand that they are the ones that ultimately control what and who influences the lives of their children and youth. This responsibility includes deciding the friends their children have, what media their children are listening to and watching, and who will be helping them with their children's education. Parents must carefully answer the following questions when they choose people to whom they will delegate some aspect of their children's education.

1. What are you doing in your home to make sure that the influences in your children's lives are Christ honoring?
2. Are the people that you associate with and allow to have an influence on your child likeminded in the faith or are their lives in conflict to biblical values?
3. Does the school your children attend meet the biblical qualifications necessary for wise delegation of your parenting responsibilities?
4. Do the leaders and teachers in your church that have influence on your children fear God, love truth, and hate covetousness? Give evidence that this is true. If it is not true, what steps do you need to take to correct this?
5. What strategies and actions do you need to develop and implement in order that you choose the right people to delegate some of your children's education to?

Engaging Churches

The church has a major impact on the hearts and minds of its children and youth. Since the church is made up of imperfect but redeemed individuals, church leaders must make sure that they select teachers that will meet the biblical qualifications for helping parents with the education of their children.

1. Does the church have an intentional, ongoing plan to disciple and equip those individuals who will be teaching children and youth? What should this plan entail and how will it be implemented throughout the church's ministries?
2. Does the church do extensive background checks and ongoing training to make sure that teachers and leaders fear the Lord and have a vibrant walk with Him?
3. What can the church do to be able to provide support to parents with the education of their children and youth?

Transforming Schools

Many times, young people spend more time under the influence of teachers and coaches, than of their parents. The school must select and train teachers, coaches, and staff members to understand their role as biblical influencers of children and youth. Schools must be intentional in hiring and developing all staff members to be strong Christ followers.

1. What hiring policies and procedures does the school follow so that only likeminded, Bible-believing staff members are selected to work at the school?
2. Is there a process in place that assures communication and behaviors of all staff members are above reproach when interacting with children and youth?
3. Are parents encouraged to be fully engaged in the everyday life of the school and is there honest, open, and frequent communication between staff and parents?
4. What actions does the school take to make sure that all staff members understand and embrace the principles of Kingdom Education™?

Chapter 8

The End Result

A teacher affects eternity; he can never
tell where his influence stops.[28]
HENRY B. ADAMS

I have learned that there is only one guaranteed result of all education. I think everyone would agree that no one can guarantee that every child will be able to achieve the same grades as all other students in a class. If someone promises that all students will achieve a certain academic standing in any class, it means that the standards must be lowered to the person with the least ability.

It is also impossible to guarantee that every child will attain the same physical skills as all other children through the educational process. This is because every child is created by God with different skills and abilities.

---

28 "Henry Adams Quotes," https://www.brainyquote.com/quotes/ henry_adams_108018.

Can you imagine if a teacher would promise that all students in her class would achieve the same fine arts abilities when the class is completed? I know that I could never get an A in choir. That is because I don't have the vocal talent needed to achieve such a grade.

Since these results can't be promised to every student, then what guarantee can education make for every student? There is only one guaranteed end result of all education. That guarantee is that the child, when fully educated, will go out into life having developed a worldview; which leads us to the eighth principle of Kingdom Education™.

Biblical Principle of Kingdom Education™ #8
The education of children and youth results in the formation of lifestyles or worldviews that will be patterned after the belief systems or worldviews of their teachers.

> *A disciple is not above his teacher, but everyone who is perfectly trained will be like his teacher.*
>
> *Luke 6:40*

> *The things which you learned and received and heard and saw in me, these do, and the God of peace will be with you.*
>
> *Philippians 4:9*

Every person develops a worldview or an underlying belief system that drives his or her attitudes and actions in life. A person will have one of two worldviews; it will be either a God-centered or man-centered worldview. Another way to categorize one's worldview is either being biblical or secular.

All worldviews consist of beliefs and assumptions about what choose to trust in life. In his book, *Inklings on Philosophy & Worldview,* Matt Dominguez builds on James Sires work to highlight seven essential questions that each of us answer in determining the worldview that acts as the lens through which we see the world. These questions are:

1. What is real?
2. Who or what is God?
3. Who am I?
4. What is the basis for right and wrong?
5. What happens when I die?
6. What is the purpose of history?
7. What is the purpose of human existence?[29]

From these seven questions, one can see the basic components of all worldviews. Every worldview is based on one's view of God, creation, mankind, moral order, purpose, knowledge, and the future. What a person believes about each of these components will shape one's worldview.

Twenty years ago in *Kingdom Education*™, I presented a pyramid that is divided into three parts—beliefs, values, and actions. The model illustrates how our beliefs shape our values which, in turn, drives our actions. We only *do* what we *believe*! Actions always follow beliefs. One's beliefs are what we often refer to as a worldview.

---

29 Matthew Dominguez, *Inklings on Philosophy and Worldview.* (Carol Stream, IL: Wander, 2020).

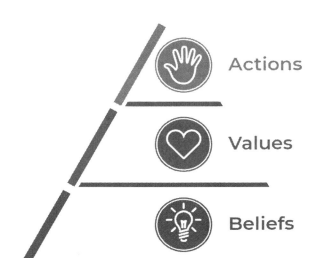

In recent years, I began asking myself where do our beliefs come from? In other words, if beliefs are the foundation of our values, then what is the foundation of our beliefs?

The result, was the realization of another level at the base of the model. This foundational level is identified as "Trust." Our perspective and understanding of reality forms our perception of what is and what is not worthy of our trust. This does not mean that as a society everything that we choose to trust is true, but our perception of truth influences our beliefs. In fact, the more I reflect on this concept, I am convinced that each one of us puts what we consider to be truth at the foundation of our lives. What we consider to be truth is what ultimately determines what we choose to trust. The result forms our system of beliefs which in turn shape our values and drive our actions.

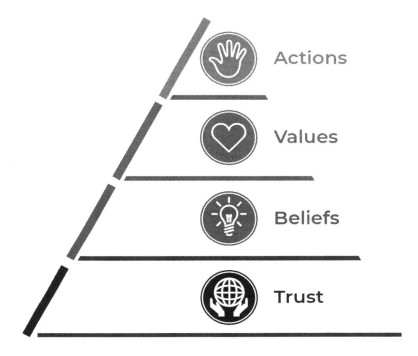

Another word used to describe our perception of truth is worldview. Our worldview is the lens of what we trust to make sense of reality as we perceive it. Our worldview impacts every aspect of our life, including the education that we provide our children and youth. If every action or form of education is based on a system of values which are based on a doctrine of beliefs that are formed by what we trust and how we view the world, then there can be no such thing as neutral education!

I can clearly remember when my professor in one of my graduate classes made the following statement: "A teacher should never share his/her personal beliefs or values when teaching students. You must teach neutrally." As soon as I heard him say this, I raised my hand. "Sir, I think that it is impossible to teach neutrally."

The professor responded with a challenge that I wasn't expecting. He told the class that we were halfway through the semester. Then, he asked me to share one of his personal beliefs or values that he had taught in any of our classes.

At first, the thought went through my mind to simply take back my remark and be quiet so I could simply pass the class. However, I told the professor that he was a devoted evolutionist. To which he challenged me to show the class when he taught that he was an evolutionist in class. Before answering, I asked him the simple question, was he?

The professor answered that it was true that he believed in evolution but that he never taught this personal belief of his in class. I respectfully disagreed. He proceeded to challenge me to show where he had done so. I had taken careful notes throughout this class, and my practice was to date my notes so I knew when certain topics were covered.

I went back through my notebook and told the professor that on a certain date he stated the following.

> *Education became necessary when man stopped using all four limbs in locomotive motion and began using the upper two limbs in simple machine motion.*

I proceeded to show the professor that I had written next to this statement that he was an evolutionist. He queried me as to how his statement said that he believed in evolution. I responded that he didn't say that this was one theory or that some people believe this. He stated it as fact. It was what he believed.

This principle was understood in the 1800s by theologian Robert L. Dabney. In his treatise on secular education, Dabney wrote,

> *The natural heart is carnal, and naturally inclines away from the gospel. To the young person, inspired by his studies, his teacher is often like a god…in a word, to the successful pupil under an efficient teacher, the school is his world. Make that godless, and his life is made godless.*[30]

This principle not only applies to the teacher in the classroom but also to the textbooks used. We must never forget that every book is written by a person or a group of people. Since every person has a worldview and cannot teach neutrally, that means that an author cannot write neutrally. His/her worldview will be communicated through what he/she writes. Author, Kevin Swanson, makes this point clear when he stated,

> *The worldview maintained by those who write the textbooks and present the curriculum does bear a lasting impact on children.*[31]

Every teacher, whether it is an individual, a parent, church leader, educator, coach, etc., influences a child in three ways. Every teacher influences a young person by:

- What one says—CONTENT
- How one says it—COMMUNICATION
- How one lives—CONDUCT

---

30   Robert L. Dabney, "Secularized Education," http://www.thecontinuingwitness.com/uploads/9/8/2/3/98238342/rld_secularized_education.pdf.

31   Swanson, *Upgrade*, 169.

I illustrated how these three influences of every teacher relate to one another in the model that is shown below.

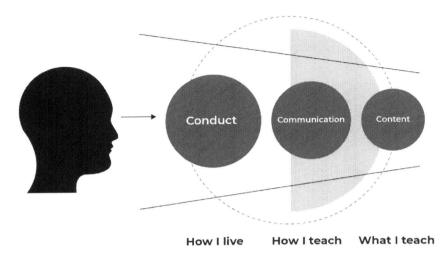

How I live   How I teach   What I teach

The Influences of a Teacher

Keep in mind when looking at this model is that the child looks through one's conduct and communication to get to the content that is being taught. If the content does not align itself with the teacher's conduct and communication, the child will reject the content and accept and model the teacher's conduct and communication.

It is critical to understand that a teacher's worldview/beliefs shape his/her conduct and communication. If the teacher has a secular worldview, that worldview will influence the young person even if the content is truthful and accurate.

Paul understood the power of these three influences that a person has when teaching others. This is why he wrote,

*The things which you **learned** and **received** and **heard** and **saw** in me, these do, and the God of peace will be with you.*

Philippians 4:9

Frank Gaebelein summed up this principle in his book, *The Pattern of God's Truth.*

> *The fact is inescapable: the worldview of the teacher, insofar as he is effective, gradually condition the worldview of the pupil. No man teaches out of a philosophical vacuum. In one way or another, every teacher expresses the convictions he lives by, whether they be spiritually positive or negative.* [32]

Parents, church leaders, and educators must develop a biblical worldview. Then they must make sure that others who might teach their children and youth do likewise. Future generations will always have a worldview that is like that of their teachers.

Think About It

Restoring Individuals

Every Christian must know, understand, and develop a biblical worldview that drives his/her thoughts, words, and actions. Christians must realize that the only guaranteed result of one's education is the development of a worldview. In order to meet this challenge, Christians must give careful attention to certain questions.

---

32   Frank Gaebelein, The Pattern of God's Truth (Chicago: Moody Press, 1954), 37.

1. Do you have a good understanding of what a biblical worldview is and how you can pass it on to others? Explain your responses.
2. What are you doing to renew your mind that will strengthen your biblical worldview?
3. Do you have a biblical understanding of God, truth, humanity, right and wrong, purpose, knowledge, and the future?

Empowering Parents

Parents must understand that their children's worldview will likely be firmly established by their teen years. They must realize that the main business of all education is the communication of ideas which will in turn shape the child's worldview. It is critical for parents to develop a strong, biblical worldview themselves so that they can pass it on to their children.

1. Have you undertaken the effort to renew your mind by taking every thought about every area of life captive to God's Word? How has your thinking changed by going through this process?
2. Are you constantly working on strengthening your worldview to make sure it is biblically based? Give evidence that this is taking place.
3. What priority is it to you that your children's education must lead them to develop a biblical worldview that will drive their actions and attitudes? What evidences are there that proves this is one of your top priorities for your children's education?
4. Are you more concerned about the academics, athletic programs, fine arts programs, etc., than you are about the worldview that your children are developing?

Engaging Churches

Church leaders must understand that every message, communication, and activity either reinforces a biblical worldview or leads children and youth to develop a nonbiblical one. The communication of a biblical worldview must be the driving force behind what the church teaches and does throughout all of its ministries.

1. Do all church leaders understand that one's worldview informs every educational effort that is undertaken?
2. Does the church conduct biblically based training for all staff and lay leaders and teachers that will help them develop a biblical worldview so that they can pass it on to others? How is this done? Give evidences that it is effective.
3. Is the church biblically addressing all the issues that children and youth will be confronted with throughout the entire educational process that they will go through?
4. What strategies and actions need to be developed to help parents develop a biblical worldview so that they will be equipped to bring their children up in *the nurture and admonition of the Lord*?
5. What is the church doing to identify and destroy secular worldviews and dualistic compartmentalizing of life in its staff, lay leaders, and teachers?

Transforming Schools

Christian schools must understand that the only end result of all education is the development of a worldview. Students will form either a secular/man-centered worldview or a biblical/God-centered one. There is no spiritual neutrality in the educational process. Careful consideration and constant examination must be done to assure that students are taught from a biblical worldview perspective.

1. What is the school doing to make sure that all staff members understand that the only guaranteed result of education is the development of a worldview?

2. How is the school helping all staff and board members to not only know what a worldview is, but also how to develop and strengthen their own worldview?

3. Does the staff understand that all textbooks are written from either a secular or biblical worldview perspective? If so, how does a biblical worldview inform the staff on textbook selection?

4. What evidence does the school have to demonstrate that students graduate from high school having developed and embraced a biblical worldview for their lives?

5. What does the school's website communicate are the school's top priorities? Is it mainly focused on academics, athletics, fine arts, or does it also include and emphasize biblical worldview development as foundational?

6. What is the school doing to partner with parents to make sure the home and school are focused on shaping a biblical worldview in the lives of all students?

Putting the Pieces Together

Every decision we make reflects our worldview.[33]
JAY STRACK

WHEN ONE STUDIES SCRIPTURE, one will discover that gaining knowledge is good, but it isn't enough. In several passages, we are instructed to go after understanding and wisdom. Proverbs 4:5 states that *we should seek and pursue wisdom at all costs.*

But how does one go about obtaining understanding and wisdom? The answer to this question is found by applying the ninth principle of Kingdom Education™.

---

33   Jay Strack (@Jstrack007), Twitter, May 5, 2020.

Biblical Principle of Kingdom Education™ #9
The education of children and youth must lead to true wisdom by connecting all knowledge to a biblical worldview frame of reference.

> *Get wisdom! Get understanding! Do not forget…Do not forsake her, and she will preserve you; love her, and she will keep you. Wisdom is the principal thing; therefore get wisdom.*
> *Proverbs 4:5*

> *The fear of the Lord is the beginning of wisdom, and the knowledge of the Holy One is understanding.*
> *Proverbs 9:10*

> *The heavens declare the glory of God; and the skies above show His handiwork.*
> *Psalm 19:1*

> *For since the creation of the world His invisible attributes are clearly seen, being understood by the things that are made, even His eternal power and Godhead, so that they are without excuse…*
> *Romans 1:20*

> *…in whom [Christ] are hidden all the treasures of wisdom and knowledge.*
> *Colossians 2:3*

There are three components of all education—knowledge, understanding, and wisdom. We see these three components mentioned throughout Scripture. To understand the difference between the three aspects of education and their relationship with each other, consider the following chart.

	Knowledge	**Understanding**	**Wisdom**
Focus	Facts	Meaning	Application
Objective	Information	Principles	Worldview
Discipline	Memory	Reason	Action

The first aspect of education is the need to gain knowledge. When this is taking place, the child gains facts in order to have correct information. In order to gain knowledge, the child primarily uses the discipline of memorizing.

The next component of education is understanding. The child needs to gain knowledge, but the focus now changes from only gaining facts to grasping the meaning associated with the knowledge. The objective is to develop principles that can be applied to all areas of life. To obtain understanding, one must use the discipline of reason. Memorization is not enough to bring about understanding.

Finally, the progression moves from understanding to gaining wisdom. Again, one must first have the needed knowledge and the understanding of that knowledge in order to advance to having wisdom. The focus of wisdom is on application and the objective is to develop a worldview that drives all of one's attitudes and actions. The discipline needed for this aspect of education is action. It is time to put all of one's knowledge and understanding into action.

There is one more thing that must be added to this chart. We need to understand what result is produced by each aspect of education. The complete chart would look like this.

	Knowledge	**Understanding**	**Wisdom**
Focus	Facts	Meaning	Application
Objective	Information	Principles	Worldview
Discipline	Memory	Reason	Action
Product	*Scholars*	*Teachers*	*Disciples*

If the education we give our children and youth focuses primarily on the gathering of knowledge, we will produce scholars. They will be individuals who know a lot of facts about a lot of different subjects. However, they will not have the ability to reason and apply their knowledge to everyday life.

When education gives equal attention to both knowledge and understanding, we will see these young people going into adult life with the ability to teach others what they know. In order to teach any subject, an individual must not only know the subject matter but must also understand the meaning behind the knowledge he/she has acquired.

The ultimate goal of education must be to develop disciples. A disciple knows the facts, has grasped the meaning of the facts, and can apply the facts to all aspects of life. It is important to understand that this progression is true for any educational effort—whether it be secular or biblical in nature.

The reality is that all education is aimed at making the next generation disciples of someone or something. What determines the type of disciple that an educational system is attempting to produce? It is determined by the worldview the teacher(s) hold. In order to develop future generations into disciples of Jesus Christ, it requires all of their teachers to have a biblical worldview and teach within the context of it.

In her book, *Total Truth*, Nancy Pearcey states,

> *We must begin by being utterly convinced that there is a biblical perspective on everything—not just on spiritual matters...The fear of some 'god' is the beginning of every proposed system of knowledge...God is the sole source of the entire created order. No other gods compete with Him;*

no forces exist on their own; nothing receives its nature or existence from another source. Thus, His Word, or laws, or creation ordinances give the world its order and structure... there is no philosophically or spiritually neutral subject.[34]

When a parent's or teacher's worldview influences a child's worldview development, we say that worldview integration takes place. We must understand that the main business of all education is the communication of ideas or worldviews. The question is not, "Will worldview integration take place in the education of a child?" The more accurate question is, "What worldview will be integrated in our children's education?"

To illustrate this, consider the following diagram.

WORLDVIEW PROGRESSION

Worldview
↓
Philosophy of Education
↓
Integration of Ideas

A person first develops a worldview. The worldview that is developed has a major influence on the person's philosophy of education. One's worldview and philosophy of education will determine what ideas or worldview he/she will integrate into every teaching moment.

---

34   Nancy Pearcey, *Total Truth: Liberating Christianity from Its Cultural Captivity* (Wheaton, IL: Crossway Books, 2004), 44-45.

I want you to consider three quotes by different educators. I am sharing these quotes in the order that I believe they will actually take place. The first quote is by Nancy Pearcey from her book, *Total Truth*. She writes,

> *The fear of some 'god' is the beginning of every proposed system of knowledge.*[35]

By the phrase "proposed system of knowledge," Pearcey is talking about any formal educational process. She is suggesting that there is a fear or reverence of some type of god behind any educational effort.

The second quote is by the late Dr. Neil Postman in his book, *The End of Education*. Postman was a secular professor of education and he noted this about all education.

> *Behind every educational effort is the pursuit of a 'god' or 'gods.'*[36]

Postman believed that anyone who is trying to educate someone else is pursuing some god or gods. I see a progression starting to take place from these two quotes. What one fears or holds in high esteem is what one pursues.

The final quote was made by two Australian Christian educators in their book, *Reclaiming the Future*. In this book, Lambert and Mitchell make this observation.

> *Every kind of teaching and learning is based upon and oriented by a shared vision of life, and that all people...*

---

35   Pearcey, *Total Truth*, 45.

36   Neil Postman, *The End of Education* (New York: Vintage Books, 1995), 84.

serve some 'god' or 'gods' in their lives and, in turn, are transformed into the image of their gods.[37]

Lambert and Mitchell make several profound points in this quote. First, when they say that all teaching and learning is grounded and influenced by a "shared vision of life," they are talking about a worldview. Second, they explain how everyone serves some god as a result of his/her education. Finally, the end result that comes from education is that students will be transformed into the image of the gods that they have been taught to serve.

Here we see the complete progression that takes place in all educational efforts. There is a "god" that is feared or held in high esteem. This god is then pursued throughout the educational process. As this god is feared and pursued, it will eventually be served by those being taught. Once this god is served, it won't take long before the student will be conformed into the image of that god.

Who or what are our children and students being conformed to? The answer to this question is found by observing what image of a god or gods they have been conformed to. Those are the god or gods that their education has taught them to fear, pursue and serve.

God created the entire universe as an expression of who He is (see Psalm 19:1-3; Romans 1:20). This means that the education we give our children and youth must not merely give them knowledge but must lead to understanding and true wisdom by causing them to see the intentional revelation of their Creator in everything they study.

---

37   Ian Lambert and Suzanne Mitchell, *Reclaiming the Future: Australian Perspectives on Christian Education* (Sydney: CSAC, 1996), 9.

Think About It

Restoring Individuals

The current culture believes that the answer to all our problems is more education. Most educational efforts focus on the gaining of knowledge. Christians must understand that God wants us to gain understanding and wisdom as we increase in our knowledge of any subject. As Christians strive to gain understanding and wisdom, certain questions must be addressed.

1. Do you see education as a process to merely increase your knowledge of something?
2. Have you been deceived into thinking that knowledge can be spiritually neutral? What evidences can you point out that supports your answer?
3. What are you doing and what can you do to gain understanding and wisdom as you increase in knowledge?

Empowering Parents

Parents need to bring their children up in the nurture of the Lord. In order to do this, parents must develop a biblical worldview in their own lives and then guide their children to gain understanding and wisdom by connecting everything they learn to a biblical worldview framework. The following questions are designed to help parents be successful in this task.

1. As you increase your knowledge, are you gaining understanding and wisdom by seeing the knowledge through a biblical worldview framework?

2. What are you doing on a regular basis to develop and strengthen your worldview to make sure it is biblical?

3. How are you helping your children understand the knowledge that they are learning within the context of a biblical worldview? Give some specific examples and show how this leads your children to have understanding and wisdom.

4. Is the education your children are receiving at school and church teach every subject within the context of a biblical worldview? Explain your response by giving specific examples.

Engaging Churches

The church's mission is to make disciples of all nations. This requires that the church teach and preach the whole counsel of God. The church must teach its members sound doctrine. However, it must also lead them to think biblically and be able to gain understanding and wisdom in everything they learn. These questions need to be addressed.

1. Is the church teaching sound, biblical doctrine through all of its ministries? Evaluate how effectively this is occurring in each of the church's ministries.

2. How does the church guarantee that teachers don't just teach Bible facts but thoroughly instruct members in the meaning of the truths and how these truths are to be applied in their everyday lives?

3. What is the church doing to help parents develop a biblical worldview so that they can instill this in their children's lives?

Transforming Schools

Much of the education that takes place in schools is focused on students increasing their knowledge in a variety of subjects. There is often an emphasis on leading students to engage in higher level thinking exercises. However, the key to effective education is when students gain understanding and wisdom as they increase their knowledge base. We know that in Christ are "hidden all the treasures of wisdom and knowledge." There are certain questions that educators must answer if the school is going to equip students with a biblical worldview.

1. How does the school effectively move students from learning facts to application of knowledge?
2. How does the school not only produce scholars but also teachers and disciples?
3. What is the school doing to equip all teachers, coaches, and sponsors with a biblical worldview and philosophy of education?
4. What is the school doing to assist teachers to be able to connect the subject matter to a biblical worldview framework?

Chapter 10

Blurred Vision

The only thing worse than being blind
is having sight but no vision.[38]
HELEN KELLER

EVER SINCE 9TH GRADE, I have had to go in for regular eye exams. I have what is referred to as myopia, which is nearsightedness. The eye doctor writes out a prescription that I use to order contact lenses. The lenses that I wear are bifocal, and I have to wear them to correct my faulty vision. When I have these corrective contact lenses in, I can see clearly things that are both close up and in the distance.

The majority of people have some form of vision impairment. They suffer from either myopia (nearsightedness) or hyperopia (farsightedness). Physical vision impairment is quite common. However, everyone suffers from some vision shortcomings spiritually. One's spiritual vision is the focus of the tenth principle of Kingdom Education™.

---

38   "Helen Keller Quotes," https://www.brainyquote.com/quotes/
helen_keller_383771.

Biblical Principle of Kingdom Education™ #10
The education of children and youth must have a view of the future that includes the eternal perspective.

If then you were raised with Christ, seek those things which are above, where Christ is, sitting at the right hand of God. Set your mind on things above, not on things on the earth.
Colossians 3:1-2

And whatever you do, do it heartily, as to the Lord and not to men, knowing that from the Lord you will receive the reward of the inheritance; for you serve the Lord Christ.
Colossians 3:23-24

Do not lay up for yourselves treasures on earth, where moth and rust destroy and where thieves break in and steal; but lay up for yourselves treasures in heaven, where neither moth nor rust destroys and where thieves do not break in and steal. For where your treasure is, there your heart will be also.
Matthew 6:19-21

These all died in faith, not having received the promises, but having seen them afar off were assured of them, embraced them and confessed that they were strangers and pilgrims on the earth.
Hebrews 11:13

For I am already being poured out as a drink offering, and the time of my departure is at hand. I have fought the good fight, I have finished the race, I have kept the faith. Finally, there is laid up for me the crown of righteousness, which the Lord, the righteous Judge, will give me on that Day, and not to me only but also to all who have loved His appearing.

2 Timothy 4:6-8

But none of these things move me; nor do I count my life dear to me, so that I may finish my race with joy, and the ministry which I received from the Lord Jesus, to testify to the gospel of the grace of God.

Acts 20:24

Most Christians have become very temporal minded. They suffer from spiritual myopia. We must keep in mind that when someone is nearsighted, it means that everything close up is quite clear. However, anything we look at in the distance is blurry.

This is the problem we have when we suffer from spiritual myopia. When we look at life in the immediate future—1-5 years—everything seems quite clear. But when asked what the future holds 20-30 years from now, things become blurry, and we don't have clear vision.

There are some Christians who suffer from spiritual hyperopia. When a person is farsighted, things in the distance are clear but anything that is right in front of them cannot be clearly seen. When applying this eye disease to our spiritual lives, we may clearly see what it will be like when we enter eternity and are in the presence of God. However, these Christians cannot discern the current times; thus, everyday life is a blur.

Whether someone suffers from spiritual myopia or hyperopia, these conditions become very serious when it comes to the education we give to future generations. Futurist Alvin Toffler noted how important it is that adults have a correct view of the future when it comes to educating their children and youth. In his treatise, *Psychology of the Future*, Toffler wrote,

> *All education springs from some image of the future. If the image of the future held by society is inaccurate, its educational system will betray its youth.*[39]

If you recall from an earlier statement, all education is future-focused. A parent teaches his/her young child to tie his shoes for one reason. The parent understands that one day the child will be on his own without Velcro and needs to know how to tie his shoes.

Toffler's treatise was written in the late 1960s. At that time, computers were items that you could only find in large corporations. Toffler envisioned a future where technology would be very advanced and would impact everyone's life. He was challenging educators to teach with an image of the future that included high tech.

His warning was that if the educational systems of the day did not include that type of vision of the future, they would be betraying the youth. When the young people matured and entered a future dominated by technology, they wouldn't be prepared.

It is even more dangerous to have an image of the future that only includes life here on earth. If Christians don't have an image of the future in the forefront of their minds that includes an eternity with a real heaven and hell, any education that they provide their children will betray them. Why? Because it will only prepare them for temporal life on earth—not eternity!

---

39   Alvin Toffler, "The Psychology of the Future," *Readings in the Socio-Cultural Foundations of Education*, edited by Burbach, Hackett, McMahon, and Wagoner (Sarasota, FL: Omni Press, 1974), 126.

Secular education denies that there is life after death. This life, here and now, is all there is. Applying Toffler's reasoning to this worldview means that secular education has a false image of the future and, therefore, it will betray its youth.

Parents, church leaders, and educators must teach their children and youth in such a way that they are preparing them not only for this life but also for eternity. A biblical education provides our children with the corrective lenses needed so that they can see their future in light of eternity.

Think About It

Restoring Individuals

One's natural tendency is to focus on the here and now. However, the Bible continually tells us that we are to live our lives within the context of eternity. The following questions are offered to help you evaluate your vision for all of life.

1. As you examine your life, what do you focus on the most? Career? Retirement? Entertainment? Friendships/relationships? Church? Growing in Christ? Serving Others?
2. How clear is the vision you have for your life 20 or 30 years from now? Do you see your immediate future quite clearly but everything is somewhat blurry beyond 5-10 years?
3. When others look at my life, do they see someone who is focused on this life or eternity?

Empowering Parents

Every parent wants their children to succeed in life. Parents invest a great amount of time, energy, and money into making sure their children's future is secure. Parents have the responsibility to provide for their children's basic needs of life. The parents' view of the future will play a big role in how they educate their children. The following questions will help parents evaluate how they are viewing the future as it relates to the education of their children.

1. Do you want your children to have the best education possible? Why? Be specific with your response.
2. Where do you want your child to be in 10,000 years because that is where he/she will be for eternity?
3. As you educate your children at home, are you doing so with eternity in mind? Explain how you are doing this.
4. Does what your children learn at church cause them to view their lives as eternal souls? Give examples of how this is happening.
5. Does the school your children attend have a view of the future that includes eternity and a real heaven and hell? If not, is that education betraying your children by not preparing them for the real future?
6. Do your words and actions tell your children that the things of this world are most important? Or do they teach your children that eternal riches and rewards are of highest priority to you?

Engaging Churches

The church is the Bride of Christ, and Jesus will return for His church one day. The Bible says that when Christ returns, He wants to find a spotless bride. The education that the church provides for its members, especially children and youth, should focus on preparing them for eternity. This responsibility requires careful attention be given to these questions.

1. How is the church preparing its members for eternity? Be specific in how this is being accomplished throughout all of its ministries.
2. Does the church consistently teach and preach the important doctrines related to heaven and hell, the soon return of Christ, the fading of the things of this world, and the importance of laying up treasures in heaven in all of its ministry endeavors? Carefully evaluate each of the church's ministries as to the thoroughness of the teaching of these truths.
3. What is the church doing to assist parents to develop an eternal mindset as they educate their children?

Transforming Schools

There are so many subjects that schools are required to teach their students. Toffler was correct when he stated, "all education springs from some view of the future." Educators must continually evaluate the view of the future that shapes all the educational efforts made. Some questions that will help schools in this evaluation are presented below.

1. If someone views the school's website and promotional material, what will they see as the primary focus of the school? The temporal or the eternal? Explain your response in as much detail as possible.
2. What does the school do to help all school constituents develop a view of the future that is framed in an eternal perspective?

3. What would the school have to change in its programs if it had a view of the future that includes a real heaven and hell for all of eternity?

4. How does the school prepare students physically for life and eternity? Socially? Mentally/intellectually? Spiritually?

Chapter 11

First Things First

Disregard the study of God, and you sentence
yourself to stumble and blunder through this
life blindfolded, with no sense of direction and
no understanding of what surrounds you.[40]
J. I. PACKER

I HAVE A QUESTION TO ASK EACH READER. If you
could only teach your child one thing, what would it be? I have asked
a similar question to administrators and teachers in Christian schools.
That question is, "What is the most important knowledge that you want
all your students to know?" Of course, when I am asking these types
of questions in a spiritual setting, I will always get a spiritual answer.

After a time of discussion, I will ask these Christian educators what
the school's parents would say if I asked them, "What does the school
believe to be the most important knowledge that all students should

---

40   J. I. Packer, *Knowing God.* (Downers Grover, IL: InterVarsity Press, 1973),
14-15.

know?" An even better place to find the answer to this question is to visit the school's website. What knowledge is being promoted on the school's site as being of primary importance.

The answer to the question "What is the most important knowledge for every child to obtain through their education at home, church, and school?" is found in the eleventh principle of Kingdom Education™.

Biblical Principle of Kingdom Education™ #11
The education of children and youth must have as its primary focus the increase in the knowledge of God.

The heavens declare the glory of God, and the firmament shows His handiwork. Day unto day utters speech, and night unto night reveals knowledge. There is no speech nor language where their voice is not heard. Their line has gone out through all the earth, and their words to the end of the world.
Psalm 19:1-4

For since the creation of the world His invisible attributes are clearly seen, being understood by the things that are made, even His eternal power and Godhead, so that they are without excuse.
Romans 1:20

Oh, the depth of the riches both of the wisdom and knowledge of God! How unsearchable are His judgements and His ways past finding out! For who has known the mind of the Lord? Or who has become His counselor? Or who has first given to Him and it shall be repaid to Him?

For of Him and through Him and to Him are all things, to who be glory forever. Amen.

Romans 11:31-36

Therefore I also…do not cease to give thanks for you, making mention of you in my prayers: that the God of our Lord Jesus Christ, the Father of glory, may give to you the spirit of wisdom and revelation in the knowledge of Him.

Ephesians 1:15-17

…that He would grant you, according to the riches of His glory, to be strengthened with might through His Spirit in the inner man, that Christ may dwell in your hearts through faith; that you, being rooted and grounded in life, may be able to comprehend with all the saints what is the width and length and depth and height—to know the love of Christ which passes knowledge; that you may be filled with all the fullness of God.

Ephesians 3:25-19

… until we all come to the unity of the faith and of the knowledge of the Son of God.

Ephesians 4:13

And this is eternal life, that they may know You, the only true God, and Jesus Christ whom you have sent.

John 17:3

Yet indeed I also count all things loss for the excellence of the knowledge of Christ Jesus my Lord…that I may know

Him and the power of His resurrection, and the fellowship
of His sufferings.

Philippians 3:8,10

For this reason we also…do not cease to pray for you, and
to ask that you…may walk worth of the lord, fully pleasing
Him, being fruitful in every good work and increasing in
the knowledge of God.

Colossians 1:9-10

…but grow in the grace and knowledge of our Lord and
Savior Jesus Christ.

2 Peter 3:18

…search for her [wisdom] as for hidden treasures; then
you will understand the fear of the Lord, and find the
knowledge of God.

Proverbs 2:4-5

Hear the word of the Lord, you children of Israel, for the
Lord brings a charge against the inhabitants of the land:
there is no truth or mercy or knowledge of God in the land.

Hosea 4:1

For those desiring to discover our purpose in life, knowing God must
be at the top of our list. Who would know and understand the purpose
of the creature other than the Creator? Or, to consider it another way,
how can we discover our purpose apart from the one who created us?

My people are destroyed for lack of knowledge. Because you have rejected knowledge, I also will reject you from being priest for Me;

Hosea 4:6

Therefore my people have gone into captivity, because they have no knowledge.

Isaiah 5:13

When I first read these verses, the thought went through my mind that the Israelites were not well educated. Did this mean that they didn't know anything? Those thoughts quickly disappeared from my thinking after I visited the Holy Land. On that visit, I saw the intricate water systems that Israel had developed. I was amazed at their engineering skills when I saw the massive stone walls that they built around Jerusalem. The Israelites were a very learned people.

So, what does it mean when the Bible says that God's people were destroyed and taken into captivity for lack of knowledge? When you study those verses in their context, you clearly see what God is saying. In Hosea 4:1, God said that there was *no knowledge of God in the land*. The same thing was true in relation to what Isaiah said. God's people were destroyed and taken captive not because they didn't know anything, but because they didn't know what was really important. They didn't know God!

God wants to be known! This is the foundational message of the Bible. Think about it. God created the universe as an expression of who He is (Psalm 19:1-3; Romans 1:20). Then, He created man in His image. Why? So that man would be able to know God and give Him the glory due Him.

Even redemption is tied to knowing God. John 3:16 tells us that everyone who believes on Jesus has eternal life. If you are born again, you have eternal life right now. If that is true, take a minute and write down your definition of eternal life. Did you define eternal life as merely living forever in heaven with God? If that is your definition of eternal life, you can't have it now because you are not in heaven with God.

Jesus defines eternal life in his prayer to the Father before going to the cross. Jesus said in John 17:3 that *this is eternal life that they may know You, the only true God, and Jesus Christ whom you have sent.* Redemption restores man's ability to know God!

I have been fascinated to see what God's motivation was in His miraculous works that are recorded throughout the Bible. God empowered David to kill Goliath, He sent fire from heaven at Elijah's request, God saved the Israelites from the Egyptian army at the Red Sea—all for one purpose. That purpose was so that everyone would *know that there is a God in this world.*

J. I. Packer in his book, *Knowing God*, sums up man's existence this way.

> *Once you become aware that the main business you are here for is to know God, most of life's problems fall in place of their own accord.*[41]

Another purpose of a Christ-centered, Bible-based education is to lead future generations to know God. Romans 1:20 has been a defining verse for me throughout my teaching career. Here, God's Word tells us that we can know and understand God's very nature by studying what He has made. Every subject a child encounters at home, church, and school

---

41   Packer, *Knowing God*, 29.

comes from some aspect of God's creation. So, Romans 1:20 applies to every area of study.

The late Dr. Albert Greene explains this so well in his book, *Reclaiming the Future of Christian Education.*

> *We must avoid the impression that academics represents the fulness of what school is all about. Knowing God in and through the creation is what is important. It brings no honor to the Holy Spirit if we then proceed to treat the ordinary school studies, which are derived totally from the created world, as if they had nothing to do with God. They are laden with meaning because they are all **part of God's way of giving Himself to us, of making Himself known to us**.*[42]

God's highest priority for mankind is for man to know Him. God made this abundantly clear when He spoke through the prophet Hosea.

> *For I desire goodness; and not sacrifice; and the **knowledge of God** more than burnt offerings.*
>
> *Hosea 6:6*

Christians throughout history understood that this was the primary purpose behind all educational pursuits. Consider what Jonathan Edwards wrote.

---

42 Albert Greene, *Reclaiming the Future of Christian Education* (Colorado Springs, CO: ACSI, 1998), 37, 44-45.\

> *Of all the knowledge that we can ever obtain, the knowledge of God, and the knowledge of ourselves, are the most important.*[43]

We live in a world where we have lost the meaning of what it is to be human. With all the gender confusion that is bombarding our children and the loneliness that our young people are facing, the only hope to understand who we are is to know God. This is because we have been created in His image. So, knowing Him is the only way to know ourselves.

Edwards went on and made this statement.

> *He who does not know Him, knows nothing else as it truly is.*[44]

Knowing God gives true meaning to all other knowledge that one can learn. In the 1600s John Milton summed up the end or purpose of education this way.

> *The end of education is to repair the ruins of our first parents; to **know God aright**, to love Him, to be like Him, to imitate Him.*[45]

This principle of Kingdom Education™ is so important. As we challenge our children and youth to gain knowledge, we must never forget that the primary focus of the education we give them must be on the increase

---

43   Jonathan Edwards. *AZQuotes.com* (Wind and Fly LTD, 2021). https://www.azquotes.com/quote/353567, accessed 2021.

44   https://www.allchristianquotes.org/quotes/Jonathan_Edwards/3049/.

45   John Milton, "Of Education," in *Basic Writings in Christian Education*, edited by Kendig Brubaker Culley, (Philadelphia: The Westminster Press, 1960), 24.

in the knowledge of God. I close this chapter with the words of Dr. S. M. Lockridge.

That's My King! Do You Know Him? [46]

Think About It

Restoring Individuals

We live in a world where an individual can consume as much information as they want through social media, the internet, and other media outlets. Christians must make it a priority to know God. It is important to evaluate our priorities when it comes to increasing our knowledge.

1. How much time do you spend trying to increase your knowledge of current events?
2. How does that compare with the time spent on knowing God?
3. Where do you go to increase your knowledge of God? Books about God? Books about Creation? God's Word? Which one of these do you spend the most time studying?
4. As you grow in your knowledge of God, how has that impacted all areas of your life?

Empowering Parents

Parents must develop habits that will increase their knowledge in many different areas and subject matters. Growing in knowledge is important in order to survive life here on earth. God's Word commands us to grow

---

46 "That's My King!" https://thatsmyking.wordpress.com/words/.

in the knowledge of God. Knowing God must be a high priority in our lives and in the education we give our children.

1. How well do you know God? Do you merely know about God or are you developing a personal, intimate relationship with Him?
2. Are you passionate about making sure your children know God as you teach them at home? Is your child's salvation of highest priority in your home? Explain how this is accomplished in your home.
3. How much time and effort do you put in to having family times of Bible study where your children can grow in their knowledge of God?
4. Based on your parenting efforts, what knowledge do your children believe you hold as most important for them to learn?
5. How does your church and school demonstrate that the most important knowledge they want your children to learn is knowledge of God?

Engaging Churches

The church teaches its members a lot of knowledge on a lot of topics. However, the highest priority a church should have for their members is to continually be increasing in their knowledge of God. This emphasis needs to be continually evaluated to make sure it maintains its priority.

1. What priority does increasing in the knowledge of God have for each of the church's ministries? Give specific examples and evidence for your response.
2. How does a church leader's knowledge of God impact his/her ministry?

3. What is the church doing to help its staff grow in their knowledge of God?
4. Evaluate how well the children and youth in the church are growing in their knowledge of God.

Transforming Schools

The major focus of most schooling is on the students increasing in what they know. Students are graded according to the knowledge they achieve. Schools must never forget that its primary focus must be focused on students increasing their knowledge of God. Schools must constantly evaluate their priorities when it comes to what they want all students to know.

1. The most important thing that every student needs to know is the saving knowledge of Jesus Christ. With that being said, is the Gospel central to the school's educational programs? How is the Gospel central to the teaching of the various academic subjects? To athletics? To fine arts?
2. If someone were to visit the school's website or view its promotional materials, what would they determine the school to believe is the most important knowledge for all students to learn? Would it be the knowledge of God?
3. How is the school ensuring that all staff understand that the highest priority of learning must be that the students are increasing in their knowledge of God?
4. Does the school communicate to the parents that the knowledge of God is supreme and at the heart of everything it does? How is this done?
5. How does the study of every subject taught at the school help students increase in their knowledge of God?

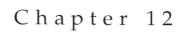

Chapter 12

It Is Not A Dirty Four-letter Word

Work was never intended to be a necessary evil, but a response to our calling and the use of our God-given skills and abilities to the glory of God and the betterment of others.[47]
RICHARD BLACKABY

CHRISTIANS BELIEVE THAT GOD CREATES each person with specific gifts and abilities in order to accomplish His unique purpose for that person's life. It is often said that there are no two people that have been created identically just like no two snowflakes are alike. Pastor James McMenis tells people that they are a "purpose with a name."

---

47   Richard Blackaby (@richardblackaby), Twitter, September 2, 2019.

What is the role education plays in helping a young person know God's will for his/her life and the work that he/she is supposed to perform? The twelfth principle of Kingdom Education™ addresses God's call on an individual's life and the work he/she is to perform.

Biblical Principle of Kingdom Education™ #12

The education of children and youth results in performing work in fulfillment of God's will for their lives.

> *Then God said, "Let Us make man in Our image, according to Our likeness; let them have dominion over the fish of the sea, over the birds of the air, and over the cattle, over all the earth and every creeping thing that creeps on the earth"… Then God blessed them and God said to them, "Be fruitful and multiply; fill the earth and subdue it; have dominion over the fish of the sea, over the birds of the air, and over every living thing that moves on the earth."*
>
> *Genesis 1:26,28*

> *Trust in the Lord with all your heart, and lean not on your own understanding; in all your ways acknowledge Him, and He shall direct your paths.*
>
> *Proverbs 3:5-6*

> *A man's steps are of the Lord; how then can a man understand his own way?*
>
> *Proverbs 20:24*

> *Your kingdom come. Your will be done on earth as it is in heaven.*
>
> *Matthew 6:10*

But seek first the kingdom of God and His righteousness, and all these things shall be added to you.

Matthew 6:33

Therefore, do not be unwise, but understand what the will of the Lord is.

Ephesians 5:17

For you have need of endurance, so that after you have done the will of God, you may receive the promise.

Hebrews 10:36

Now may the God of peace…make you complete in every good work to do His will, working in you what is well pleasing in His sight, through Jesus Christ.

Hebrews 13:20-21

For this reason we also…do not cease to pray for you, and to ask that you may be filled with the knowledge of His will in all wisdom and spiritual understanding; that you may walk worth of the Lord, fully pleasing Him, being fruitful in every good work.

Colossians 1:9-10

I beseech you therefore, brethren, by the mercies of God, that you present your bodies a living sacrifice, holy, acceptable to God, which is your reasonable service. And do not be conformed to this world, but be transformed by the renewing of your mind, that you may prove what is that good and acceptable and perfect will of God.

Romans 12:1-2

As we examine this principle, please note that I will be using the terms "God's will" and "God's call" interchangeably. Whatever call God puts on one's life must be in accord with God's will for that person. Throughout Scripture, God wants each person to know His will for their lives.

God told Jeremiah that He knew him and had a purpose for him before he was even being formed in his mother's womb.

> *Before I formed you in the womb I knew you; before you were born I sanctified you; I ordained you a prophet to the nations.*
>
> *Jeremiah 1:5*

David said the same thing when he wrote the 139th Psalm. God knows each one of us and has a perfect will for each of us to perform while we are here on earth. God also wants each of us to know His will or His call on our lives. Paul explains why God wants us to renew our minds in Romans 12. The reason why renewing our minds is so important is so we can prove God's perfect will for our lives.

The education we give our children and youth must lead them to recognize God's call on their lives. This has to be part of the educational process at home, church, and school and must begin at the earliest age possible. Author, Kevin Swanson, makes a powerful point in his book *Upgrade.*

> *A successful education is achieved when a child is prepared to make maximal use of his God-given talents and abilities in the accomplishment of the child's calling...Everybody is*

> *gifted and has a purpose in God's world…Each child has a*
> *specific calling framed by his unique talents and abilities.*[48]

Author and pastor, Dr. Tim Keller, explains how a person can discover God's call on his/her life. In his book *Every Good Endeavor*, Keller writes,

> *The way to find your calling is to look at the way you were*
> *created.*[49]

Swanson explains the major challenge facing every parent, church leader, and educator when it comes to educating young people.

> *The challenge of the first eighteen years of a child's education*
> *is to find that calling [God's will] … A fulfilled life will*
> *be determined by whether he/she has centered in upon his*
> *or her life calling.*[50]

The reason why it is so important to help every child identify God's calling on his/her life is because every person has been designed by God to work. This is clearly understood in God's cultural mandate He gave to man when He first created him.

> *Then God blessed them and God said to them, "Be fruitful*
> *and multiply; fill the earth and subdue it; have dominion*
> *over the fish of the sea, over the birds of the air, and over*
> *every living thing that moves on the earth."*
>
> *Genesis 1:28*

---

48 Swanson, *Upgrade*, 13, 17.

49 Tim Keller, *Every Good Endeavor* (Penguin Books, 2012).

50 Swanson, *Upgrade*, 14.

Work is not a dirty four-letter word. It is really a divine concept. This is because God is a God who works. We see His work of creation that He performed when He spoke the world into existence in six days.

We are told in Genesis that after He created the heavens and the earth, He rested on the seventh day. Genesis 2:2 records *that on the seventh day God ended His **work** which He had done, and He rested on the seventh day from all His **work** which He had done.* Since God is a God who works and we are created in His image, that means that each and every person has been designed to work.

Author Eric Metaxas made an interesting observation in a Breakpoint article. He said,

> *That worldview says that God created the universe out of nothing, that He has set up a series of observable, rational laws to govern it, and that mankind—male and female—has been created in His image with the God-given ability to discover things about the physical world and bring order and blessing to it. As the eminent historian Rodney Stark has written, "Christian theology was necessary for the rise of science."*[51]

Man has been given the unique ability to understand God's creation ordinances by which He governs His creation so that man can perform work for God's glory. Discovering one's talents and abilities and honing them so that they can be used to perform work must be a major focus of the education we give children and youth.

---

51   Eric Metaxas, "BreakPoint: Scientists and Christianity," https://breakpoint. org/, January 23, 2018.

Unfortunately, we have lost the biblical concept of work. At one time, work was equated to one's vocation that God called one to perform for His glory. Then, work became a job that man would ask God to bless. Over time, work simply became a job one performed to get ahead and pay the bills. I recently read that work is now defined as the "ability to consume."

There are two books that I highly recommend to Christians to read. One is Tim Keller's book *Every Good Endeavor*. The second book is Darrow Miller's book *LifeWork*. These two resources can equip parents, church leaders, and educators to better help young people develop a biblical view of work.

Keller challenges Christians to

> ...*recover the idea that work is a "vocation" or calling, "a contribution to the good of all and not merely...a means to one's own advancement... to one' self-fulfillment and power.*"[52]

He goes on to define what he means by the term, vocation.

> *Something can be a vocation or calling only if some other party calls you to do it, and you do it for their sake rather than your own. Our daily work can be a calling only if it is reconceived as God's assignment to serve others.*[53]

Darrow Miller explains work as a measure of God's calling when he wrote,

---

52   Keller, *Every Good Endeavor*, 2.

53   Ibid. 55.

He [God] has given us seven days a week and fifty-two weeks a year. This time is to be used to build lives that honor the Creator, enhance His creation and create culture that reflects God and His created order.[54]

As we educate our children and youth, we must help them identify their God-given abilities. Then, we must guide them in their search for God's call/will on their lives. Finally, we must provide them with the education necessary for them to develop their abilities in order to perform work in fulfillment of God's call on their lives. Puritan leader William Perkins sums this principle up with these words.

The main end of our lives…is to serve God in the serving of men in the works of our callings.[55]

Think About It

Restoring Individuals

Every Christian must understand that God created them in His image and has a plan for his/her life. You are a purpose with a name. God instills within every individual certain gifts and abilities in order for that person to fulfill His will or call on one's life. Christians need to continually seek to find and follow God's call on his/her life.

1. What gifts and skill sets has God given to you?

---

54 Darrow L. Miller, *LifeWork: A Biblical Theology for What You Do Every Day* (Seattle, WA: YWAM Publishers, 2009), 158.

55 Leland Ryken, "The Original Puritan Work Ethic," *Christian History Magazine* 89 (2006), https://christianhistoryinstitute.org/magazine/article/original-puritan-work-ethic.

2. How do these talents and abilities help you to find His call on your life?

3. In what ways are you performing work as unto the Lord for His glory?

4. Do you view your work as a job you have in order to pay bills or as God's calling on your life that is an act of worship when you perform that work? Explain how you see your work as your ministry.

Empowering Parents

Most parents want their children to get a good education so that they will hopefully get a good job and have a successful life. However, Christian parents must understand that their children have been created by God so that they can answer His call on their lives. Understanding this principle is very important for every parent as they provide an education for their children.

1. Do you view your work as God's call on your life? Do your children understand that everything you do at home and at work is your vocation to which God has called you? Give examples of how you are doing this.

2. How are you teaching your children to view their role as a student? Do they understand that being a student is God's call on their lives at this stage of life and that they are to perform this "work" for God's glory?

3. How are you leading and teaching your children to work as unto the Lord in everything they undertake in life?

4. What effort are you making to help your children identify the gifts God has given them and what His call may be on their lives?

Engaging Churches

The church's mission is to make disciples of all nations. A disciple understands his/her giftedness and has identified God's call or will for his/her life. The church must help its members understand the Creation Mandate and how God has a purpose for each person so that this mandate can be fulfilled.

1. How is the church helping all its members, regardless of age, to understand that God has a purpose and plan for their lives? How does the church guide its members to find God's call on their lives and see all work as holy unto the Lord?
2. What is the church doing to educate its members to recognize their gifts and abilities and use them to strengthen the church, the Body of Christ?
3. What is the church doing to help parents understand that parenting is part of God's call and will for their lives and they need to perform that work as a pastor fulfills his calling to shepherd the church?

Transforming Schools

God has created each individual to do work as a stewardship for some aspect of His creation. The chief purpose of education is to equip young people to live their lives in accordance with His purpose and for His glory. The education of children and youth must lead them to recognize their abilities and God's purpose/call for their lives.

1. What is the school doing to help and guide students to recognize God's call on their lives?

2. How does the school help all staff members to view their work at school as God's will for them?

3. How is the education provided by the school helping students hone their God-given talents and abilities in order that they are equipped to fulfill God's call on their lives?

4. Since God gives each individual different talents and abilities, how does the school provide training that develops each individual student? How can the school differentiate its educational programs so that each student can be equipped to fulfill his/her unique calling from God?

5. When a student graduates from high school, does he/she know how God has created him/her with specific abilities and God's call on his/her life? Give examples of how this is accomplished.

Chapter 13

Everybody Talks About It

> Comparison either puffs us up with pride or weighs us down with shame – neither are helpful or holy. Our goal isn't to be better than the next person. Our goal is to be like Christ.[56]
> BLAKE ODGERS

WE ARE SURROUNDED by the desire for excellence. Individuals claim they pursue it. Businesses claim they have achieved it. Institutions promise they will instill it.

Before we delve into the next principle, and without reading ahead, I want you to turn to the last page in this book and write down your definition of excellence.

---

56 Blake Odgers (@Blake_Odgers), Twitter.

How do you define excellence?

Now, consider your circle of influence. How does your family, your church, or your school define excellence?

Now, read your definition and ask yourself this question, "Did my definition of excellence focus primarily on performance or achievement?"

The vast majority of people, including Christians, view excellence as something that defines one's performance or achievement. The problem is that this definition illustrates the world's concept of excellence and not one that is reflective of a biblical worldview.

This is not to say that we should not be pursuing excellence. Anyone involved in education should be pursuing excellence, and we should be encouraging children to pursue excellence. But we need to ensure that the excellence we are pursuing is clearly centered on Christ.

A review of the websites of Christian school reveals our conventional concept of what it means to be excellent. Here is a sample; perhaps some of them will sound familiar to you.

- *Excellence in education speaks to the whole student, encompassing academic, spiritual and extra-curricular components*
- *Committed to academic excellence*
- *Executes a series of policies and procedures that result in academic excellence*
- *A strong emphasis on academic excellence*
- *Educating, equipping and encouraging in faith, excellence, and service*
- *To be a Christ-centered place of excellence*
- *An educational program that promotes excellence*

- *Staff should strive for excellence in all areas of their professional life*
- *A wonderful heritage of academic excellence*
- *Embracing biblical excellence*
- *Focus of all truth through excellent academics*
- *Christian values and academic excellence go hand in hand*
- *An environment of spiritual and academic excellence*
- *We value academic excellence*

Whenever I am presenting a workshop on excellence with a group of educators from Christian schools, I go to their websites and make note of what they are saying about the topic. After listing what I found, which was much like what I have listed above, I ask them if they know what these statements actually mean. I further query them as to whether everyone on staff would define these statements the same. Finally, I ask them how the parents of the school's students would interpret these statements.

The reality is that we use nice sounding statements like these but seldom define what we mean when we use them. This leaves the meaning of such statements up to each individual.

Before we look at this principle, I want to share with you various schools of thought that exist on the topic of excellence. These schools of thought will give us an idea of how the world defines and views excellence. This will not be an exhaustive look at these schools of thought but only a summary of each one.

Social Excellence

Social excellence is a commitment to the highest values of society. Excellence is described as talents and achievements which are socially useful. With society's values in an ever-increasing state of decline, the standard for excellence according to this school of thought must also become lower and lower.

Human Excellence

Excellence is related to the purpose for which something exists. A knife is excellence in relationship to its purpose for existing—its ability to cut. Human achievement is the pathway to excellence.

Personal Excellence

Success is the goal of life. Excellence is whatever produces success. The aim is for the individual to realize his/her potential.

Utilitarian Excellence

Excellence is defined as a means to an external end.

Technical Excellence

This school of thought involves the application of skills to performances and activities. The focus of excellence is primarily on acquiring certain skills and how well one can perform them.

To sum up the world's concept of excellence as explained by these schools of thought, excellence can be defined as the *perfecting of oneself, based on human ability and achievement*. Worldly excellence can be best defined with two words—compare and compete. The world's concept of excellence is strictly based on a horizontal perspective. Its goal is superiority to others and can easily result in pride.

The world's concept of excellence does not take into consideration one's character. When excellence is defined only by one's performance and achievement, we end up with a whole lot of "experts."

The problem with defining excellence in today's world is that true excellence has to do with values, ideals, and standards. Today's postmodern culture has abandoned the concept of absolute, divine standards. With no absolute standards to aim at, excellence becomes relative and cannot be measured.

In our pursuit of excellence, Christians must develop a biblical model of excellence or a model that is biblical (in a biblical model I present, one finds Christ at the center). Biblical excellence begins with a vertical perspective. With this as the starting point, a biblical model for excellence will be completely different from the world's model. Excellence from God's perspective is completely opposite of the world's concept of excellence. The difference between biblical and worldly excellence is summed up in the figure below.[57]

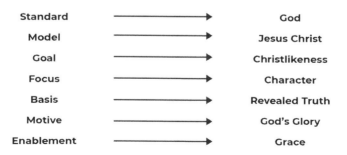

EXCELLENCE FROM GOD'S PERSPECTIVE HAS A DIFFERENT:

Standard	→ God
Model	→ Jesus Christ
Goal	→ Christlikeness
Focus	→ Character
Basis	→ Revealed Truth
Motive	→ God's Glory
Enablement	→ Grace

57   Gary Inrig, *A Call to Excellence* (Victor Books, 1985), 34-35.

Biblical excellence is not defined by what God does but by Who He is. Because God is excellent in His person, everything He does is excellent. This must be our focus as we educate our children and youth and challenge them to pursue excellence.

Does a biblical model of excellence disregard performance? The answer is no. When pursuing biblical excellence, one's performance becomes an extension of one's character. Dr. Gary Inrig has done considerable study on the concept of biblical excellence. He summarizes the congruency of performance and character this way.

> *Character development is the key to usefulness…excellence of character rather than excellence of achievement must be the central concern of the believer…the priority of character is due to the fact that what a person is colors all that he does.*[58]

This same perspective is captured by Darrow Miller in his book *LifeWork*. Miller writes,

> *Because redeemed man is working for God, to fulfill God's plan, the work is to be done with excellence.* **Our guidelines for excellence are found in God's own nature.** *God is true, just, and beautiful. Our work, in both its means and ends, is to manifest truth, justice, and beauty.*[59]

Embracing a biblical model for excellence is found in the thirteenth principle of Kingdom Education™. It reflects the correct relationship between performance and character when pursuing excellence.

---

58   Inrig, *A Call to Excellence*, 74.

59   Miller, *LifeWork*, 160.

Biblical Principle of Kingdom Education™ #13

The education of children and youth must be characterized by the pursuit of biblical excellence based on godly character resulting in competent performance.

> *For we dare not class ourselves or compare ourselves with those who commend themselves. But they, measuring themselves by themselves, and comparing themselves among themselves, are not wise.*
>
> *2 Corinthians 10:12*

> *And this I pray, that your life may abound still more and more in knowledge and all discernment, that you may approve the things that are excellent, that you may be sincere and without offense till the day of Christ, being filled with the fruits of righteousness which are by Jesus Christ.*
>
> *Philippians 1:9-11*

> *Finally, brethren, whatever things are true, whatever things are noble, whatever things are just, whatever things are pure, whatever things are lovely, whatever things are of good report, if there is any virtue and if there is anything praiseworthy—meditate on these things.*
>
> *Philippians 4:8*

> *But you, O man of God, flee these things and pursue righteousness, godliness, faith, love, patience, gentleness.*
>
> *1 Timothy 6:11*

> *O Lord, our Lord, how excellent is Your name in all the earth, who have set Your glory above the heavens.*
>
> *Psalm 8:1*

Whatever your hand finds to do, do it with your might.

Ecclesiastes 9:10

Again, we must remember that worldly excellence is based on a horizontal perspective. It is summed up by the words compare and compete. One is excellent from the world's perspective if he/she is better than someone else or defeats someone else. This is not what God expects out of His people. Paul warned the Corinthian church about the danger of comparing themselves by themselves. He said that when one measures himself by others, that person is not very wise (2 Corinthians 10:12).

We must pursue excellence because God is excellent and we are to reflect Him in all we are and do. When God speaks of excellence, it is always in relation to His character and not His deeds. The education we give our children and youth must pursue biblical excellence that is based on godly character. When that happens, they will perform at their best. Why? Because they are representing Jesus Christ and that demands our best.

Think About It

Restoring Individuals

Every Christian's life should be marked by excellence. This is because God is a God of excellence. However, Christians must be careful to pursue excellence that is defined from a biblical perspective. As you strive for excellence, consider the following questions.

1. How do you define excellence by how you are currently pursuing it?

2. Are you determining excellence in your life by comparing your life to others?

3. What role does competition play in your pursuit of excellence?

4. What changes do you need to make in your life in order to pursue excellence that follows a biblical model? To move from a performance and achievement model to one based on godly character?

Empowering Parents

Parents must pursue excellence in their personal lives as a model for their children to follow. However, we must challenge our children to pursue biblically defined excellence versus what the world considers to be excellent. This requires a thorough evaluation of our concept of excellence in light of God's Word.

1. How are you as parents modeling excellence to your children?

2. Has your pursuit of excellence been based on one's performance or achievement as the defining factor as to whether one is excellent or not?

3. Does the education that your children are receiving at home, church, and school challenge them to pursue biblical excellence? How is this taking place at home? At church? At school?

4. Are you challenging your children to develop godly character that will cause them to perform to their best ability as a testimony of Christ?

Engaging Churches

The church should model biblical excellence because it represents the Body of Christ. It is true that everything that is done at church should be done with excellence. Facilities should reflect excellence. However, the church must pursue excellence of character first and foremost. This requires church leaders to consider several key questions related to the church's pursuit of excellence.

1. To what extent is the church defining excellence by comparing itself to other churches or the world?
2. How is the church instilling excellence in its members that is defined biblically?
3. What changes need to take place for the church to model biblical excellence that has as its primary goal to be Christlike, and is pursued with the motive to glorify God?

Transforming Schools

Schools have always challenged its students to pursue excellence. There is the drive for the school to be marked by academic excellence. Every coach challenges his/her athletes to strive for excellence and perfection. However, much of the emphasis on excellence in schools is modeled after the world's concept of excellence. Schools need to evaluate their pursuit of excellence to ensure that it follows the biblical model found in this principle of education.

1. When a person visits the school's website, tours the campus, attends athletic events, or receives communication about the school's programs, will he/she see that school pursues excellence in everything?

2. Is the school's pursuit of excellence based on a horizontal perspective defined by comparison and competition? Is the driving force behind its pursuit of excellence the desire to be better than other schools and beat the competition? Give specific evidence that supports your response.

3. What reputation does the school have in areas such as athletics and other activities where there is competition with other schools? Do students, coaches/sponsors, and spectators display Christlike character at all times?

4. What strategies does the school need to develop and implement in order for the school to strive for biblical excellence in its operations and develop biblical excellence in the lives of its students?

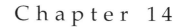

Chapter 14

Finding Purpose

Education is the nurture and development
of the whole man for his proper end.[60]
ROBERT L. DABNEY

AS WE EDUCATE FUTURE GENERATIONS, it is critical
that we understand God's ultimate purpose for education. Knowing
purpose is extremely important. It has been said that:

> *Without purpose, one loses hope;*
> *Without hope, one dies;*
> *Or merely exists!*

This is not only true for an individual but it is also true for an
organization. When a home, church or school loses its purpose, it will
eventually die. Even if it doesn't die completely, it will only exist. I have

---

60   Dabney, "Secularized Education," http://www.thecontinuingwitness.com/
uploads/9/8/2/3/98238342/rld_secularized_education.pdf.

137

seen schools that have drifted from God's purpose and they merely were going through the motions and the routines of being a school.

To understand God's purpose for education, one must first understand God's purpose for one's life. In order to understand God's purpose for one's life, one must understand God's purpose for why anything and everything exists.

Knowing God's ultimate purpose for everything that exists is the focus of the fourteenth principle of Kingdom Education™.

Biblical Principle of Kingdom Education™ #14
The education of children and youth must equip them to fulfill God's highest purpose for man to glorify Him and enjoy Him in life and eternity.

> *For of Him and through Him and to Him are all things, to whom be glory forever.*
>
> *Romans 11:36*

> *For by Him all things were created that are in heaven and that are on earth, visible and invisible, whether thrones or dominions or principalities or powers. All things were created through Him and for Him. And He is before all things, and in Him all things consist.*
>
> *Colossians 1:16-17*

> *I am the Lord, that is My name; and My glory I will not give to another*
>
> *Isaiah 42:8*

Do you not know that your body is the temple of the Holy Spirit who is in you, whom you have from God, and you are not your own? For you were bought at a price; therefore glorify God in your body and in your spirit, which are God's.

1 Corinthians 6:19-20

Therefore, whether you eat or drink, or whatever you do, do all to the glory of God.

1 Corinthians 10:31

The heavens declare the glory of God; and the firmament shows His handiwork.

Psalm 19:1

For since the creation of the world His invisible attributes are clearly seen, being understood by the things that are made, even His eternal power and Godhead.

Romans 1:20

Who [Jesus] being the brightness of His glory and the express image of His person.

Hebrews 1:3

Then God said, Let Us make man in Our image, according to Our likeness…so God created man in His own image; in the image of God He created him; male and female He created them.

Genesis 1:26-27

I have addressed God's purpose behind His creating the heavens and the earth earlier in this book. It is extremely important for us to not only know the what and how about God's creation but also the why behind it. Since this is so vital to all of life, it bears repeating again. This time I will go into the why behind creation in greater depth as it relates to this principle.

We learn from Scripture that God is eternal both in His person and nature. He did not need any aspect of creation in order to be more God. However, God decided to express His glory by creating the heavens and the earth. We see this in Psalm 19:1-3 and Romans 1:20. When you read in Genesis 1 the words, *Let there be*, you can paraphrase it as *This is who I am*. Let there be light becomes I am light. Creation is an expression of God's person and nature.

God's Word also makes it clear that God not only expressed Himself by creating the heavens and the earth but He also did it for one purpose— His glory! Romans 11:36 and Colossians 1:16-17 declare that everything was created by Him and *for Him*.

Imagine what it must have been like halfway through day six of creation. The universe was all in place. The seas were teeming with fish, and the sky was filled with birds of amazing variety. The dry ground was the habitat of every beast of the ground. The grandeur of God's creation was on full display. It was even more glorious than when Isaiah saw the Lord sitting on His throne and the seraphim were crying out, *holy, holy, holy the whole earth is filled with His* glory.

But there was something missing. Sometimes my imagination begins to run wild when I am studying God's Word. During one of those times, I wondered if God the Father said to His Son and Holy Spirit, "look at what we have created. Our glory fills the earth." Was it at this point that the Father said, "we aren't finished yet. There is one more creation act that must be performed. We are going to create one more being and he will be called man."

I can imagine God continuing, "Man will be different from all other created beings, and he will be the crown jewel of Our creation." Genesis 1:26-27 records this discussion. God said,

> Let Us make man in Our image, according to Our likeness…so God created man in His own image; in the image of God He created him; male and female He created them.

Here is the climax of creation—man being created in God's own image. Why was this necessary? Remember that God created the universe so He would be known and glorified. Before man was created, God's glory was on full display, but none of the other created beings had the ability to both know God and give Him glory.

This all changed when man was created in God's image. Man was a relational being as a reflection of a relational God. Man had a mind to study, reason, discover, and analyze all of creation. He was the epitome of God's purpose for creation—for God to be known and glorified.

I find it fascinating that after God created man, male and female, in His image, the very first command he gave them was to *be fruitful and multiply and fill the earth*. Why did God command man to do this? Because God wanted image bearers of Him all around the world so that there would be someone who could know God and give Him glory.

Dr. Tony Evans explains this in his series, *Raising Kingdom Kids*.

Be fruitful and multiply and fill the earth with children –
why? Because man was created in the image of God. So the
goal of having children is the replication of God's image,
not just the replication of your image...so the purpose of
children was the replication of God and the advancement
of God's kingdom in history.[61]

Of course, we know that the Fall brought death and destruction into God's creation. Man's spirit died and he no longer could know God. However, because of God's grace, God sent His Son to earth as a man. Jesus would live a sinless life and then lay His life down on the cross and die for mankind's sin.

Whenever a person puts his/her faith in the death, burial, and resurrection of Jesus Christ as payment for his/her sin debt, he/she inherits eternal life. According to John 17:3, eternal life restores man's ability to know God and, thereby, be able to give Him glory.

This is eternal life, that they may know You, the only true
God, and Jesus Christ whom You have sent.

So, God's ultimate purpose for every person is for him/her to intimately know God and glorify Him in everything that he/she thinks, says, or does. This is clearly stated by Paul in 1 Corinthians 10:31.

...whether you eat or drink, or whatever you do, do all to
the glory of God.

---

61   Dr. Tony Evans, "Raising Kingdom Kids," sermon series *The Kingdom Family,* preached at Oakcliff Bible Church, Dallas, TX.

The question becomes, what does it mean to glorify God? We have the tendency to use spiritual terms and phrases without clearly defining them.

Does one glorify God after scoring a touchdown by pointing to the sky and taking a knee? Or is it when we pray before a meal when we are in public? Or do we glorify God by sitting alone in quiet meditation on who He is? How would you define it? Is your meaning of glorifying God easily applied to all of life?

Dr. Gary Inrig explains what it means to glorify God in a way that is very practical in relation to every situation I find myself in. He explains it this way.

> *One's glory is one's reputation...God's glory is not just His reputation but His revealed character, the display of His attributes.*

> *To glorify someone therefore is to increase his reputation by revealing his true nature...**to glorify God is to live in such a way that His character is displayed and His praise is increased**.*[62]

To sum all of this up, we must understand that each person is created in God's image with the purpose of knowing God and giving Him glory. This means that the education we give our children must be aligned with God's ultimate purpose for them. Dr. Francis Schaeffer put it this way.

---

62   Inrig, A Call to Excellence, 56.

Man, made in the image of God, has a purpose — to be in relationship to God, who is there. Man forgets his purpose and thus forgets who he is and what life means.[63]

The Westminster Assembly adopted a catechism many years ago. The first question in this catechism asks, what is the chief end of man? The answer is as follows.

Man's chief end is to glorify God, and to enjoy Him forever.

This means that the main purpose of education must equip children and youth with the ability to better glorify God and enjoy Him throughout life and eternity. Therefore, the education we provide our children must guide them to develop the knowledge, skills, and attitudes (character) that will enable them to glorify God in whatever they think, say, and/or do.

Think About It

Restoring Individuals

Every person desires a life of significance and purpose. It is often difficult to find purpose in a material reality that has chosen to be separated from God and His will. However, when a Christian understands the "why" behind creation, the result of the fall and to be redeemed and restored into an understanding of God's purpose for life, then we can move forward with a vision of true significance.

1. If you were asked to write a purpose statement for why you exist, what would you say?

---

63   Francis Schaeffer, https://www.azquotes.com/quote/844228.

2. How does understanding why God created everything help you know your purpose and find significance?

3. How is fulfilling your God given purpose a struggle because of the fall?

4. How can you help others understand that God has an ultimate purpose for creating them?

Empowering Parents

One of the major tasks of being a parent is to guide children to know God's purpose for their lives. This is the ultimate goal behind every educational effort that takes place in a child's life. Parents need to understand the truths of a biblical worldview in order to teach their children to pursue God's purpose for their lives.

1. As parents, are you able to teach your children the what, how, and why of creation, the effect of the fall on one's purpose, and how redemption restores a person's God-given purpose?

2. How are you educating your children at home so that they know that God created them to know Him and give Him glory in all they think, say, and/or do?

3. Is a biblical worldview the foundation of the education your children are receiving at church? At school? If not, what are your children learning about their purpose for their existence?

4. What can you do to make sure that the education your children receive will be focused on helping them find God's ultimate purpose for their lives?

Engaging Churches

Every church needs to make sure that its members know the what, how, and why God created the heavens and the earth. In order to make disciples of all nations, the church must teach the entire biblical narrative referred to as a worldview. This is required if the body of Christ comes to fully understand God's ultimate purpose for each person's life.

1. How does the church make sure that all teachers know and understand a biblical worldview, especially why God created everything and made man in His image?
2. Is the teaching of a biblical worldview woven into the programs of every ministry of the church? What evidence is there that this is happening?
3. Are children and youth being taught that they are created in God's image and their inherent worth and intrinsic value can only be found in this truth? How is this being done throughout the church's ministries?
4. How is the church equipping parents in developing a biblical worldview and providing resources for them to instill this in the hearts and minds of their children?

Transforming Schools

School leaders and teachers must know, understand, and develop a biblical worldview in their individual lives. Understanding creation, the fall, and redemption must be a driving force behind all of the school's programs. Students must be taught that they are image bearers of God and have a unique purpose from the early grades through high school. Schools need to consistently reflect on God's ultimate purpose of education to make sure its efforts are focused on this end.

1. How does the school make sure that all staff members understand God's ultimate purpose for education by fully understanding creation, the fall, and redemption?
2. What strategies need to be developed and implemented so that the truth that every child is an image bearer of God is not merely a slogan that staff members rehearse?
3. If the school fully embraced God's ultimate purpose for education as defined in this principle, what would the school need to start doing, continue to do, and/or stop doing?
4. Are the textbooks and other instructional resources used to shape the students' hearts and minds written from a biblical worldview perspective that reinforce God's ultimate purpose for education?

Chapter 15

Moving Forward

FOR MANY YEARS, I taught a seminary-level philosophy of education course. The class met for seven hours each day for a week. At the end of the course, I had the students write a paper titled "So What?."

These students had invested an entire week of their lives in this single class. That is a lot of time. I wanted to know what difference the class was going to make in their lives. Why did they do it? What would they do with it? Was their experience going to end with a grade, or would it impact their future lives and ministry?

The fact that you are reading this chapter means that you have spent valuable hours reading this book and answering a lot of questions. You may have also read the first book in this series *Understanding Kingdom Education*™.

My question to you is the same one that I asked my students at the end of each class.

So what? What difference will *Applying Kingdom Education*™ make in your life? Your home? Your church? Your school?

I believe there are three possible answers to this very important question.

To understand these possible answers let's examine Paul's experience in Athens.

> *And they (the people of the city) took him and brought him to the Areopagus, saying, "May we know what this new doctrine is of which you speak? For you are bringing some strange things to our ears. Therefore we want to know what these things mean." For all the Athenians and the foreigners who were there spent their time in nothing else but either to tell or to hear some new thing.*
>
> *Acts 17:19-21*

Paul preached a powerful message declaring who the true God was. Those who had gathered to hear what this man had to say about these "strange" things responded in three different ways.

> *And when they heard of the resurrection of the dead, some mocked, while others said, "We will hear you again on this matter." So Paul departed from among them. However, some men joined him and believed...*
>
> *Acts 17:32-34*

Some simply mocked and rejected what they heard Paul proclaim. Others simply said that it was interesting and they would probably get back together and discuss it some more. Both of these responses resulted in no change—they were all satisfied with the status quo.

But there was one group who *joined Paul and believed*. Their lives were drastically changed forever. It is my prayer that, after reading this book, you will believe and join God by following His plan for educating future generations. If you, as a parent, pastor, church leader, and/or educator make this decision, I promise you that your life will change forever.

If you find as you have been reading and interacting with the principles outlined in this book that they have been resonating with and you believe the Holy Spirit has been stirring your heart, then I invite you to join me by taking these next steps.

I believe that these steps will position us to raise a generation that will have the opportunity to complete the task and fill the earth with the knowledge of the glory of God.

Action 1   *Repent and Cry Out to God*

In Nehemiah 1, we find Israel in captivity. A remnant from Jerusalem came to Babylon and Nehemiah questions them about the city. When he heard that the walls of Jerusalem were broken down and the gates burned, Nehemiah sat down and wept. He then prayed and fasted for days. I encourage you to read Nehemiah 1 and see how he saw his sin and the sin of Israel, and repented and begged God to forgive him. He then prayed that God would allow him to rebuild the walls of Jerusalem.

We find ourselves in a very similar situation. We, too, are in captivity. As Erwin Lutzer puts it in his book, *Church in Babylon, We are exiles, not geographically, but morally and spiritually.*[64] The walls of our homes and churches are broken down and our gates burned.

---

64   Erwin Lutzer, *The Church in Babylon* (Chicago: Moody Publishers, 2018), 31.

I agree with Lutzer when he stated in his book, *We Will Not Be Silenced,*

> *The purpose of this book is not to inspire us to "take America back." We have crossed too many fault lines; too many barriers have proven too weak to withstand media-driven cultural streams that have flooded our nation…I write not so much to reclaim the culture as to reclaim the church.*[65]

We have fallen too far to return our country to what it once was. We have gotten to this place because the vast majority of Christians have allowed the world to educate their children for many decades.

However, hope is not gone. We are here and God still wants to use us to advance His kingdom. Therefore, we must do as Jesus told the church in Sardis: *"Wake Up! Strengthen what remains!"* (see Revelation 3:2).

How do we do this? We must do what Nehemiah did. We must sit down, weep, and cry out to God to forgive us for our complacency. Then comes the process of rebuilding the walls of our homes and churches.

Action 2 *Build Strong Families*

When God allowed Israel to be taken into captivity, He told them to settle down and build strong families. He wanted a remnant to remain that would know, love, and serve Him; whether the nation remained in captivity or was restored. Even in captivity, the family is still the God-ordained foundational building block of all civilization.

---

65   Erwin Lutzer, *We Will Not Be Silenced* (Eugene, OR: Harvest House Publishers, 2020), 36.

To build strong families will require immediate action by every individual Christian, parent, pastor, church leader, and educator. The entire body of Christ must be committed to making the family strong again. To accomplish this will require that some additional actions take place.

Action 3   *Renew Our Minds*

One of the reasons why Christians are in captivity today is due to wrong thinking. Many Christians have developed a secular worldview that drives all of their actions and attitudes. Even those Christians who desire to live a biblically informed life, most likely have succumbed to dualism where their lives are fragmented by a sacred/secular divide.

There is little hope to adequately prepare future generations for what lies ahead if individuals, parents, church leaders, and educators don't renew their minds (see Romans 12:2). Renewing the mind and developing a biblical worldview is an everyday spiritual battle that won't end until we reach our final destination.

In order to develop a strong biblical worldview, requires every Christian to fully understand creation, the fall, and redemption.

Action 4   *Be Committed to Kingdom Education™*

God wants each of us to love Him with all of our heart, soul, and mind. When we die, the only thing we will leave behind us is the next generation. We must always remember that what God wants out of the next generation and all future ones is for them to love Him the same way He wants us to love Him.

This won't happen merely because they may be born into a Christian family or go to church regularly. It will only become a reality if all Christian adults know, understand, and commit themselves to 14 biblical principles of Kingdom Education™ (see Appendix A for the complete list).This cannot be done in a piecemeal way. It will take the whole body of Christ to accomplish this task.

It begins with individuals studying and applying these principles to their lives. As individuals are restored, parents must be empowered by these very same principles. This will also require churches to be fully engaged in the process by training parents providing the support needed for parents to fulfill their God-given responsibility to educate their children biblically. Finally, schools must be transformed into institutions that fully embrace Kingdom Education™.

It has taken many decades to get us to where we are today. It will take some time to turn the ship around. We can no longer be complacent and allow secular education to conform our children and youth to the world.

As I was writing this concluding chapter, one of KEM's senior associates sent me a quote by A. W. Tozer. Tozer not only sensed the urgency of the hour but also the danger that comes when Christians snuggle up too close to the culture.

> *Any objection to the carryings on of our present gold-calf Christianity is met with the triumphant reply, "But we are winning them!" And wining them to what? To true discipleship? To cross-carrying? To self-denial? To separation from the world? To crucifixion of the flesh? To holy living? To nobility of character? To despising of the world's treasures? To hard self-discipline? To love for God?*

To total committal to Christ? Of course the answer to all these questions is no.[66]

You are now at the end of this book. It is time to act. I heard a saying many years ago that has proven to be true in my life. It is very applicable to my purpose for writing this two-volume series, *Understanding Kingdom Education™* and *Applying Kingdom Education™*.

The road marked "TOMORROW" only leads to the city named "NEVER!"

Today is the only time to take action. It is time to move forward!

---

66 "What Are We Winning People To? – AW Tozer," https://deeperchristianquotes.com/what-are-we-winning-people-to-aw-tozer/.

Appendix A

Fourteen Essential Principles of a Biblical Philosophy of Kingdom Education

GOD'S WORD PROVIDES CHRISTIANS with principles that will guide them in how to educate future generations. These principles are:

1. *The education of children and youth is the primary responsibility of parents.*
   Deuteronomy 6:4-9; 11:18-21; Psalms 78;1-7; Psalms 127:3; Proverbs 22:6; Malachi 2:13-16; Ephesians 6:4

2. *The education of children and youth is a 24 hour-a-day, 7 days-per-week process that continues from birth till maturity.*
   Deuteronomy 6:7; 11:19; Proverbs 22:6

3. *The education of children and youth must have as its primary goals the salvation of and discipleship of the next generation.*
   Psalms 78:6-7; Matthew 28:19-20

4. *The education of children and youth must be based on God's Word as absolute truth.*
    Matthew 24:35; Psalms 119

5. *The education of children and youth must hold Christ as preeminent in all of life.*
    Colossians 2:3, 6-10

6. *The education of children and youth must not hinder the spiritual and moral development of the next generation.*
    Matthew 18:6; 19:13-14; Mark 10:13-16; Luke 18:15-17

7. *The education of children and youth, if and when delegated to others by parents, must be done so with utmost care to ensure that all teachers follow these principles.*
    Exodus 18:21; I Samuel 1:27-28; 3:1-10

8. *The education of children and youth results in the formation of a belief system or worldview that will be patterned after the belief systems or worldviews of the person's teachers.*
    Luke 6:40

9. *The education of children and youth must lead to true wisdom by connecting all knowledge to a biblical worldview frame of reference.*
    Romans 1:20; Psalm 19:1; Proverbs 4:5,7; 3:19; 9:10, Psalms 104:24; 136:5; Jeremiah 10:12; Romans 11:33; Luke 11:52; Colossians 2:3; 1 Corinthians 8:1; 13:8; Romans 1:28

10. *The education of children and youth must have a view of the future that includes the eternal perspective.*
    Colossians 3:1-2; Matthew 6:19-20; 2 Timothy 4:6-8; Acts 20:24; Hebrews 11:13; Colossians 3:23-24

11. *The education of children and youth must have as its primary focus the increase in the knowledge of God.*
John 17:3; Romans 1:20; Romans 11:33-36; Psalm 19:1-6; Ephesians 1:16-19; 3:15-19; 4:13; Philippians 1:9; 3:8-10, 13-14; Colossians 1:9-10; 2:2-3; 2 Peter 3:18; Proverbs 2:5; Hosea 4:1; 6:6; and 2 Corinthians 10:3-5

12. *The education of children and youth results in performing work in fulfillment of God's will for their lives.*
Genesis 1: 26; Matthew 6:10, 33; Ephesians 5:17; Hebrews 10:36; 13:20-21; Colossians 1:9-10; 12:1-2; Proverbs 3:5-6; 20:24

13. *The education of children and youth must be characterized by the pursuit of biblical excellence based on godly character resulting in competent performance.*
2 Corinthians 8:7, 10:12; Philippians 1:9-10, 4:8; 1 Timothy 6:11; Psalm 8:1; Ecclesiastes 9:10

14. *The education of children and youth must equip them to fulfill God's highest purpose for man to glorify Him and enjoy Him in life and eternity.*
Romans 11:36; Colossians 1:16-17; Genesis 1:26-27; Isaiah 42:8; Psalms 19:1-3; Romans 1:20; Hebrews 1:3; 1 Corinthians 6:19-20; 10:31

Made in the USA
Monee, IL
19 July 2023

39490816R00094